# NIRVANA TAO

# NIRVANA TAO

The Secret Meditation
Techniques of the
Taoist and Buddhist Masters

## DANIEL ODIER

*Translated by John Mahoney*

INNER TRADITIONS INTERNATIONAL LTD
NEW YORK

TO KHEMPO KALO RINPOCHE

*Khempo Kalo Rinpoche of the Kagyupa Order, one of the great sages who continue the teachings and oral tradition of Milarepa*

Inner Traditions International, Ltd.
377 Park Avenue South
New York, New York 10016

First U.S. edition 1986

*Nirvana Tao* was first published in French under the same title
by Editions Robert Laffont, Paris 1974.

Copyright © 1974 by Editions Robert Laffont

First English translation copyright ©1986
by Inner Traditions International, Ltd.

Library of Congress Cataloging in Publication Data

Odier, Daniel, 1945-
   Nirvano-Tao : the secret meditation techniques of
   the Taoist and Buddhist masters.

   Translation of: Nirvano Tao.
   Bibliography: p.
   1. Meditation (Buddhism)   2. Meditation (Taoism)
   I. Title.
   BQ5612.035   1986        294.3′ 443        84-15753
   ISBN 0-89281-045-9

10   9   8   7   6   5   4   3   2   1

Printed and bound in Great Britain

# T A B L E   O F   C O N T E N T S

\* \* \*
\* \*
\*

## PART ONE
## BUDDHISM

## PART TWO
## TAOISM

*Buddha, guardian of the entrance to Swayambunath, one of the great places of pilgrimage in Nepal*

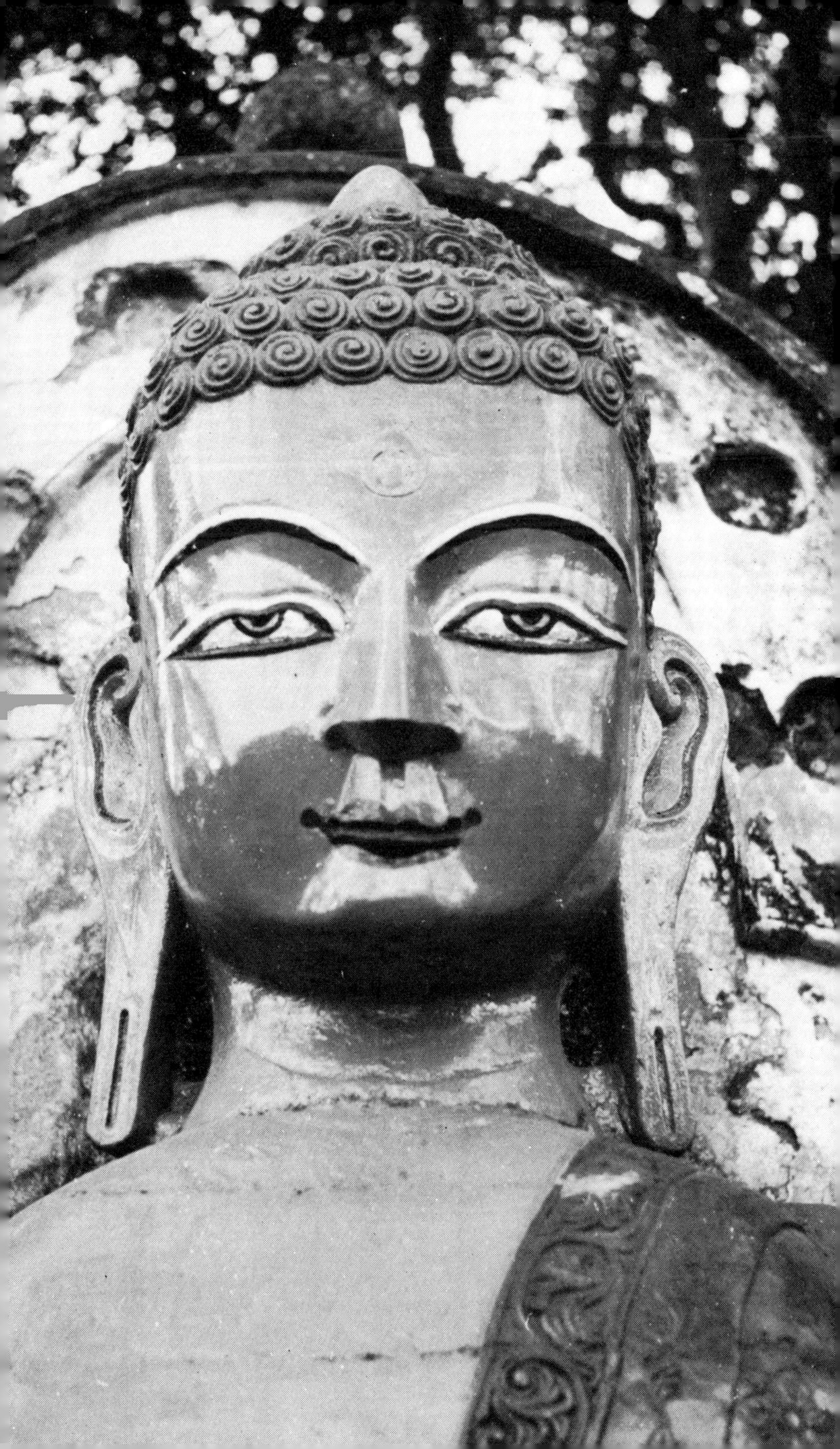

# INTRODUCTION

\* \* \*

\* \*

\*

In limiting this work to the contemplative techniques of Buddhism and Taoism, I intend to go directly to the essential and leave
aside everything that does not have a direct relationship with the
Way that leads to Nirvana and to the Tao.

Most books dedicated to Buddhism single out a particular
school. They then expose the doctrines in detail, often stopping
before treating the essential: the different techniques of meditation.

In the course of my many trips to the Orient, in the monasteries
of each school, I strove to understand and to live what the books
rarely describe in detail for the good reason that Orientalists often
prefer philosophical studies to direct experience.

In order to restore the essence of this experience, I have chosen
to treat this subject with the greatest scrutiny and clarity possible,
while at the same time preserving the integrity of my research.

The whole interest of a direct physical experience is that it
allows the setting aside of books and teachings in order to
encounter men or sages who are the realization of a complete
doctrine and whose presence is irreplaceable. This alone can
open a mind burdened with knowledge to the realization of the
void.

To meet a master, a man who says everything by his simple
presence, is to open oneself to an intense and profound upheaval
that passes like a tidal wave over all the ideas that one might
make of a doctrine.

# PART ONE

*

# BUDDHISM

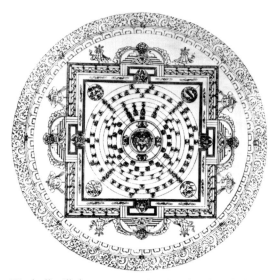

His skull will show a protrusion. His hair braided over the right shoulder will be azure. On his wide, smooth forehead between His eyebrows there will be a small, raised circle of silver hairs. His eyes, shaded by long eyelashes like those of a heifer, will be large, white and black. His ear lobes will be three times longer than normal. He will have forty solid identical teeth, which will shelter a long and slim tongue, giving him an excellent sense of taste. His jaw will have the strength of a lion's. Along with a fine, golden-colored skin, He will have a limber and firm body like the stalk of the arum, a large chest like the breast of a bull, round shoulders, solid thighs, gazelle legs and seven well-distributed protruding contours. His hands will be large. His arms, hanging, will touch his knees. His extremely long fingers and toes will be joined by a thin membrane. His hair will grow strand by strand, and the hair on His arms will grow upward. What needs to be hidden will remain so. His heels will be thick, and His palms will be united. Under each of His feet a thousand-spoked wheel will be traced, and He will stand perfectly upright on symmetrically equal feet. And His speech will have the sound of that of Brahma.[1]

\* \* \*

\* \*

\*

## CHAPTER ONE

# THE LIVES OF THE BUDDHA

Some definite statements can be made concerning the life of the Buddha through careful research, in-depth study, comparison of original texts, and information obtained from archaeological research.

The Buddha was born in 556 B.C. in a small village of Nepal in the region of Tirai, Kapilavastu. He belonged to a tribe named Shakya of which his father was king. There is no information that tells us whether Buddha was an Aryan or of the yellow race. When he was about twenty-seven years old, he left Kapilavastu and became a wandering ascetic. Near the hamlet of Uruvela, in India, about a hundred kilometers from Patna, he entered a cave and practiced an extremely rigorous meditative asceticism. When he was about thirty-seven years old, he achieved Illumination and left for Benares, where he found five ascetics who became his first disciples. There he gave his first sermon, in which he exposed the Four Truths and the Way of Deliverance, the Noble Way of the Eight Paths. Buddha continued to spread his teaching to an increasing number of disciples and founded the Sangha, the congregation of monks. In the area of Patna, rich lay people allowed through their donations the development of several centers where Buddha and his disciples lived during the period of the monsoons, which made travel impossible. After a life of teaching, Buddha died at the age of eighty-one following a sickness or poisoning. The teachings of the Buddha were transmitted orally for about 400 years before being written down with commentaries in the course of the following centuries.

## THE LEGENDARY LIFE

Although the lives of the great initiators of humanity were more internal than external, their disciples were able to give a fairly accurate account of their teachings. However, their imagination had to compensate for the unknown details of the masters' lives.

Buddha did not escape from this any more than Jesus did. Everything begins with a virginal birth and culminates by a promise of a future return.

Maya-Devi, pure and radiant, marries King Shuddhodana, after a foreboding dream and a series of miraculous omens, and finds herself transported by the gods to the top of the Himalayas, where a tree shoots forth. Led into a golden palace by celestial attendants, Maya-Devi sees a yellow elephant possessing six tusks of ivory and a rosy head. After offering to the queen a lotus that he holds in his trunk, the miraculous animal stabs one of his tusks into the right side of the queen, who feels nothing.

Ten months later, the queen, hidden by a thicket of leaves, lies down at the foot of a fig tree. Instantaneously the soil is covered with thick grass from which ten thousand lotuses spring forth. Without her experiencing the least pain, the Buddha emerges from her right side. A giant lotus provides a bed for him. The Buddha rises, takes seven steps toward the north, south, east and west and takes possession of the world. He announces his last incarnation and says that he will free man from suffering brought on by birth, old age and death. As soon as the infant finishes speaking, he becomes similar to others.

Soon the young Prince Siddhartha amazes teachers and sages with the extent of his knowledge. No one is equal to him in athletics, such as horseback riding and archery. Still, the young Prince spends long hours in the marvelous gardens of the palace where, near ponds covered with lotuses, he falls into delicious contemplations. One day Siddhartha goes into the fields with his father, who has him admire the thick furrows of earth raised by the plow. The young Prince sees the beauty of the spectacle, but he also sees the suffering of the buffalo, the hardship of the laborer and the death of the worms cut by the plowshare. He sees in nature that the struggle for life means the law of the survival of the fittest. His love for each breath of life is so strong that he asks his father if he can remain where he is in order to meditate. In spite of the move-

ment of the sun, the shadow of the tree that shelters him does not
move, and Siddhartha knows his first ecstasy.

The king, impressed by the attitude of his son, remembers the
predictions of a brahman: 'Choosing the life of a wandering ascetic, he will attain Illumination after my death and will save the
world!' Had he seen the first signs of this force that would propel
his son from his realm?

Upon the king's return, he gives orders that no similar sights
that could provoke such contemplation be allowed around the
young prince. He constructs three palaces in which Siddhartha
enjoys the most refined pleasures. Sometimes, however, fleeing
his rich surroundings, Siddhartha goes into the gardens, and in a
hut made from branches he enters ecstasy.

One day, he goes to the edge of the parks and sees beyond the
ordered flower beds the wild abundance of the jungle. There, for
the first time, he meets some ascetics. What force dwells in these
beings with a look more luminous than precious jewels?

The king, aware of the melancholy of his son, thinks that it is
time to find him a wife. He seeks out the most beautiful young
women of his caste, who are presented to the Prince during a
feast. Among the 108 candidates, each more beautiful than the
other, only the last, Gopa Yasodhara, attracts the attention of Siddhartha.

'As the hidden seed springs up from the soil after a long dryness,
their former love awoke immediately. They had already been
united so many times, man and woman, tiger and tigress, vine and
orchid, wind and feather, mountain and river . . . .

'A meeting of the minds: no need for him to remember the fawn,
which for her sake, he had caught in the forest, and no need for her
to remember the storm, which for thirty-three days had detained
them, drunk with love, in a cave overhanging the swollen river. As
long as the wheel of rebirth kept turning, that which had been
would continue to live in them.'[2] After conquering his rivals in the
different tests of running, the bow, the sword and contests of
learning, Siddhartha marries the beautiful Gopa. In three months,
the king builds a palace even more beautiful than the preceding
ones so that Gopa and the Prince can taste the most intense sensual pleasures. At night, the craftsmen construct a wall around the
paradise so that the Prince is surrounded by a vortex where everything is youth and beauty. The king gives these orders: everything
that can be perceived as sickness, aging and death must be kept

from his son. As soon as a dancer shows the least sign of fatigue, she must be immediately replaced. There is neither withering flower, dead leaf, nor flickering lamp within the walls of the palace.

Soon Gopa learns that she is going to give birth to a son. Siddhartha himself, in the midst of a vision, sees the meaning of his mission on earth. The Prince orders his carriage to be harnessed and asks to depart into the city, which is then garlanded with flowers. Old people and slaves are hidden from him, and the entire realm is transformed into a place of happiness and beauty. Then, all of a sudden, in front of his carriage, appears a repulsively ugly human being at the threshold of death.

During the night, Siddhartha, by disguising himself, escapes into the village and sees it in its usual condition. He sees a funeral convoy that he follows to the place of cremation. The body rises up in the middle of the flames and firewood, and the skull explodes in the stench of burnt flesh. When the Prince returns, the entire palace is seized by weariness: flowers do not open, musical instruments are silent and the women seem exhausted.

Siddhartha meditates on what he has seen. He keeps Gopa at a distance from his bed, and the women, in spite of all the sensuous distractions that they are displaying in front of their beloved Prince, are not able to move him from his deep contemplation.

One evening, after having been entertained by the musicians and dancers, Siddhartha falls asleep. Toward the middle of the night, he awakes suddenly to a frightening scene. The half-asleep women look like cadavers, and the precious silks that cover their decrepit bodies are no longer anything but shreds of colorless fabric. Their mouths are open showing their rotted teeth, their skulls are bald, and a terrible odor comes from their bodies. Siddhartha rushes toward Gopa's room. She hasn't changed. Her body and face are as resplendent as ever.

At night, under the starry sky, Siddhartha leaves the palace on his white horse. He crosses the sleeping village and rapidly leaves it behind. At dawn, near the river Anoma, at the edge of the kingdom, he leaves his horse, and exchanges his princely robes for those of a hunter clothed in rags; then he cuts his braid of hair with one motion of the sword. The braid, flung into the air, is swept up into the sky and disappears.

Freed from the snares of sensual pleasures and wealth, Siddhartha goes in the direction of the Ganges plains. He crosses jungles, desert terrains, and cultivated fields; his mind, now free from every memory, opens itself to a new rapture.

After several days of travel, the Buddha arrives at the village of Vaishali, where he has come to follow the teachings of a celebrated brahman, Alara Kalama. After hearing the philosopher's subtle doctrine in which everything has a fixed place, Siddhartha challenges his teachings:

'You have not at all penetrated my heart because I have found neither compassion for suffering nor a way to remedy it. It is the liberation of man that I seek, and you, you do not even care whether man's plight is changed. You do not seek anything but power and only the subjugation of the gods is important to you.'[3]

Later, he meets a sage that the faithful come to see from all over Asia whom the disciples say is the incarnation of Rama. Siddhartha, after listening to the sage Uddaka, says to him:

'I am convinced, my venerable Master, that the path you expose will not lead me to indifference to the attractions of the world, nor to the detachment of the passions, nor to the serenity of the soul. I will find there no end to the vicissitudes of being. Therefore, my wandering must continue until I find the true way.'[4]

Five men follow the Buddha, knowing that this ascetic will guide them to the beyond. However, he has not yet attained Illumination, and it is with fierce determination that he isolates himself in a cave near Rajagriha. Forgetting about the tigers, vultures and snakes that frequent the area, he plunges himself into a rigorous asceticism that almost leads to his death. His five companions, tired of waiting for a teaching that is not yet formulated, leave the Buddha while mocking his intentions. The Sage proceeds to the area of Uruvela where the sweetness of the landscape, a green meadow situated between two rivers, the Nairanjana and Mohana, contrasts with the austerity of the cave. One day, the meeting of a zitherist inspires one of the principles of his later teachings: A very tight string will break, and a very loose string will not vibrate properly. The true way is that of the middle. It is the same for the body. Very great asceticism will destroy it, and too much pleasure will prevent it from vibrating: the true way is the way of the middle.

Once recovered from the austerities that almost lead to his death, the Buddha again begins to travel, covering several different regions.

After receiving a favorable omen, he chooses a fig tree, under

which he sits at the close of day, and decides to die where he is if
his meditation does not lead to the end of suffering. The forest animals, whose eyes only are visible at the edge of the clearing, watch
the Sage: movement and sound are stilled and the entire universe
awaits the revelation of the Buddha, who is supported by a seat of
cool grass which has grown beneath him.

There, he experiences the demonic forces of Mara, who tries to
make him renounce his task. Why save the world: is it not sufficient to save yourself? After the long parade of the demonic forces,
Mara, who cannot weaken his determination, sends Kama, God of
the sensual passions, who offers the ascetic the beauty of his own
daughters.

Mara, faced with this impenetrable determination, unleashes a
terrible storm with heavy rain and thunder and lightning in order
to disturb his meditation. Meteorites fall from the sky, and arrows
are transformed into flowers before dropping around the ascetic.

During the first night, the Sage sees five hundred and fifty past
existences. Each of them is retold in the *Jataka*, a very popular
collection of stories in Asia that is used to initiate children into the
teachings of Buddhism:

A long time ago, when King Brahmadatta ruled at Varanasi, the
Bodhisattva was reincarnated into a family of farmers. When he became
an adult, he earned his living by being a farmer.

At that time, there was a merchant who went to market with his wares
carried by his donkey. When he arrived at a certain place, he removed the
merchandise from the donkey's back, and covered the donkey with a
lion's skin, releasing the donkey into the rice or barley fields.

At the sight of the donkey, the attendants of the field said:

'It is a lion!'

And they didn't dare go near it.

Then one day, the merchant went to the outskirts of the village and
while he was cooking his morning meal, he covered the donkey with the
lion's skin and released it into the barley field. The attendants of the field,
taking the donkey for a lion, dared not go near it, and they ran to alert
everyone. All the villagers took up arms. Sounding the horn and beating
the drum, they returned to the field, making a lot of noise.

Frightened with the fear of death, the donkey began to bray. Then,
seeing that it was a donkey, the Bodhisattva delivered this first stanza:

It is not the cry of a lion,
Nor a tiger, nor a panther!
Clothed in the skin of a lion,
It is a miserable donkey who brays.

The villagers then perceived that it was a donkey, and after having broken its bones with the blows of a stick, they left with the skin of the lion.

Then the merchant arrived. Seeing his donkey who was about to die, he delivered this second stanza:

> For a long time yet this donkey
> Would have been able to graze the green barley
> Clothed in the skin of a lion
> But, in crying out, it caused its doom.

As he thus spoke, the donkey died: the merchant left it and went off.[5]

During the second night, the Buddha discovers the complexity of the universe. He sees the galaxies, the different suns, space, time, matter and the emptiness that formed it. He sees large bodies at the point of extinction, the meteors, comets, living stars and dead stars. As a rainbow unfolds in the sky, so the infinity of time unfolds before him: the past and the future, the cosmic periods of evolution and decay. Life's cycle appears to him at the cosmic level. He sees death engender life, obscurity light, and the indefinite form, in the continuity of rebirths.

During the course of the third night, the kingdom of nature and its laws appear clearly to him. The destruction of life in order to conserve life, as when his father first showed him the plow cutting

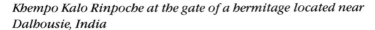

*Khempo Kalo Rinpoche at the gate of a hermitage located near Dalhousie, India*

the earth, appears to him in a different light: the lioness who kills the gazelle in order to nourish its young acts in harmony with its own nature: the bird who devours the worm and the snake who swallows small mammals do not act against their own nature.

During the fourth night, new visions spring from those that preceded, revealing suffering, and how it is the result of human life and the inseparable companion of perception. He sees man's fear of his own inner nature. While trying to escape from suffering, man indulges in sensual and mental pleasure but he only recreates a greater sorrow. Man's search lies in one direction: he wants to free himself from suffering. The ways he adopts are superficial. Even when he indulges in religion he does not find peace. Then the vision of the Four Noble Truths is revealed to the Buddha.

1. Evil is the contact of the body, the mind and consciousness, which forms the illusory view of the world.
2. The origin of evil is destiny, the cause of rebirth.
3. The cessation of evil is the cessation of desire.
4. The life that leads to the cessation of evil is that of the Eight Paths: correct view, correct intention, correct action, correct speech, correct livelihood, correct effort, correct mindfulness, correct meditation.

Next, the Buddha again goes through the Twelve Hindrances, the causes of suffering. Then, in accomplishing the inverse way, he shows the way of liberation.

The way of total deliverance is now laid out. The Buddha enters into the deepest ecstasy. Illumination frees him from ever having to suffer or be reborn.

The earth trembles twelve times, a breath penetrates the world and a light sets it aglow. At this precise moment, all evil actions cease. Everyone feels a light within. The animal world itself remains peaceful, and while the divinities rejoice, the demons lament. In her palace, Gopa knows that the Prince has arrived at the ultimate liberation.

For seven weeks, his body and consciousness remain perfectly still while Buddha is in ecstasy. However, the mischievous divinities are already tempting him to give up his teaching. His goal has been accomplished, so why remain on this earth to diffuse a message of liberation? Nirvana is waiting!

After forty-nine days, Buddha terminates his contemplation and decides to deliver to the world the secret of liberation. He seeks a man who has an elevated mind suited to a total comprehension and thinks of the sage Alara, a brahman whose teaching he had followed. But he finds out that he is dead. Then he thinks of the five disciples who were faithful to him for six years. They are at Deer Park in Benares.

The greeting he receives is cold. Has he learned anything? Then, confronted with the words of someone whose great modesty they can at least recognize, they open up to Light.

'I am the Holy, the Perfect, the supreme Buddha. Listen to me, O Monks! The way of total liberation has been found.' Then he reveals to them the Four Noble Truths, the Eight-fold Path and the hindrances of cause and effect.

It is in Deer Park at Benares that the Buddha first diffuses his teaching. Day and night, the faithful gather to hear this revolutionary message.

Soon the Buddha gathers sixty disciples. He then leaves Deer Park for Uruvela, and it is on the way that he teaches his doctrine to the three musicians, who will follow him henceforth and play ecstatic music while he preaches.

Donations from the laity provide for the establishment of two locations at Sarvasti and Rajagriha, from which the Buddha and his disciples will spread the doctrine untiringly north and south.

During his forty years of teaching, the disciples of the Buddha became more and more numerous. From village to village, with miraculous cures, the Buddha leads the men who will listen to him toward the understanding of the emptiness of the world and the emptiness of phenomena. As his disciples gradually progress, he outlines and deepens his teaching, which culminates in those practices of concentration and meditation that will be explained in detail in chapters that follow. For those who listen to him, he forges the purest instrument that man can utilize for his deliverance and shows that he himself owes the revelation of the law to meditative practices, to which he devotes himself. The considerable success that the Illuminated One has gained does not occur without arousing hatred and jealousy. Devadatta, unhappy about his defeat at the time of the competition that preceded the marriage of Gopa and Siddhartha, tries particularly hard to discredit the Master. However, his maneuvers go astray. He tries to kill the Buddha by unleashing upon him a mad elephant used to crush the heads of these who are condemned to die. But the unchained elephant becomes peaceful at the signal of the Sage.

Devadatta attempts other offensive acts, but each time he fails.

However, Devadatta is not the only enemy of the Buddha. The Jainists are also struggling against Buddhism, which is developing in a way parallel to their religion.

One day, the Perfect One receives a message that his father fears that he will die before seeing his son and profiting from his teaching. Buddha, accompanied by numerous disciples, leaves for Kapilavastu. Numbering twenty thousand, they advance slowly towards the small kingdom. All decked out, the village awaits the return of the Prince, who travels through the air at the last stage of his journey. The crowd expects an earthly king and instead see a poorly clothed man, wearied by a life of teaching and a difficult voyage. The king himself is disturbed by the appearance of his son. Only Gopa understands the glory of her husband, and that very night, as she sees him again, she attains Illumination without the Buddha having to reveal his teaching to her. (This direct transmission was rather frequent at the beginnings of Buddhism, and the Tibetans say that it is still produced today in exceptional cases when master and disciple are joined in the same emptiness.) The son of the Buddha also receives the teaching. Little by little, the other princes renounce the artificial joys of the court in order to follow the way of the Sage. The populace listen to his teaching, and many are touched by the Light. The Buddha admits women into the congregation and prescribes very strict rules for them. Before leaving Kapilavastu, he gives the law of the Five Paramita that his desiciples must observe:

'Be compassionate and respect all life, be it ever so small. Stifle in yourself hatred, greed and anger.

'Give and receive freely, but do not take anything wrongly through violence, fraud or false statements.

'Never lie even on occasions which seem to absolve you from it.

'Avoid drugs and drink, which disturb the mind.

'Respect another's wife and do not commit any illegitimate carnal act nor any unnatural act.

'These are the five rules of your life for each day.'

After having taught for forty years, the Buddha, at the age of eighty-one feels tired. He continues his teaching in spite of the onset of an illness. Near the small village of Kusinara, he lies down on the ground between two isolated trees in the middle of a field. A blacksmith prepares a meal for the monks and the Buddha. In order to honor the Sage, he serves him meat. It was this dish, legend tells us, that was the cause of the Master's death. Feeling that his end is near, the Buddha remains alone with Ananda, his preferred disciple. These are his last words as the *Mahaparanir-vanasutra* gives them:

Then, in truth, the Blessed One spoke to the venerable Ananda: 'O Ananda do not think that we no longer possess the word of our deceased Master and that we no longer have the Master. O Ananda, do not consider things of this sort. The doctrine and discipline that I have taught and commented on will be your master when I am gone. What's more, O Ananda, after my disappearance, the monks will no longer have to bow and call each other "Friend" as they do today. But a younger monk will have to be greeted by an older monk by his own name, or by his family name or by the title of "Friend". An older monk will have to be greeted by a younger monk by the title of "Venerable" or "Lord." After my disappearance, O Ananda, if the community desires it, it can abolish the secondary and minor rules.'

Then, in Truth, the Blessed One spoke thus to the monks: 'In addition, O Monks, if one of you still experiences doubts concerning the Buddha, the Doctrine, the Community, the Way or the Path, then ask me so that you will not regret it later and say:

"When our Master was here, we did not try to question him face to face."'

When he had thus spoken, the monks remained silent. Three times, the Blessed One repeated his demand, and three times the monks remained silent. He then said:

'Then in truth, O Monks, is it through respect for your Master that each of you does not question him, and speaks to one of your companions?'

The monks again remained silent. Then, in truth, the Venerable Ananda said to the Blessed One:

'It is marvelous, O Venerable One, it is amazing, O Venerable One! How confident I am in this community of monks! Not one monk experiences doubt or uncertainty concerning the Buddha, or the Doctrine, or the Community, or the Way or the Path.'

'The confidence that you express, O Ananda, is inferior to the knowledge of the Tathagata. There is truly no monk in this community who experiences doubt or uncertainty concerning the Buddha, the Doctrine, the Community, or the Way or the Path because the last of the five hundred monks has penetrated into the Truth. Consequently, he has been released from the law of rebirth into unhappiness and instead remains fixed on the Way of Deliverance and has as his goal the complete Awakening.'

Then, in truth, the Blessed One spoke thus to the monks:

'Now, O Monks, I say this to you: The components of the Self are submitted to dissolution. Strive to attain your goal diligently!'

Such were the last words of the Tathagata.

Then, in truth, the Blessed One entered the first meditation. Leaving the first meditation, he entered the second meditation . . . the third meditation . . . the fourth meditation . . . the domain of infinite space . . . the domain of infinite awareness . . . the domain of extinction . . . the domain where there is neither perception nor the absence of perception . . . the cessation of sensations and perceptions.

Then the Venerable Ananda asked the Venerable Anuruddha:

'O Venerable Anuruddha, is the Blessed One completely extinguished?'

'No, Friend. Ananda, the Blessed One is not completely extinguished. He has attained the cessation of sensations and perceptions.'

Thus, the Blessed One, having left the meditation of the cessation of sensations and perceptions, entered the domain without perception or absence of perception . . . the domain of extinction . . . the domain of the infinity of awareness . . . the domain of infinite space . . . the fourth meditation, the third meditation, the second meditation, the first meditation. Having left the first meditation, he entered the second meditation. . . the third meditation. . .the fourth meditation. . .Immediately after he left the fourth meditation, the Blessed One was completely extinguished.

As soon as the Blessed One was completely extinguished, there occurred a great trembling of the earth, terrifying and horrible, and the thunder of the divine drums burst forth.

*Khempo Kalo Rinpoche's Monastery Altar, at Sonada near Darjeeling, India*

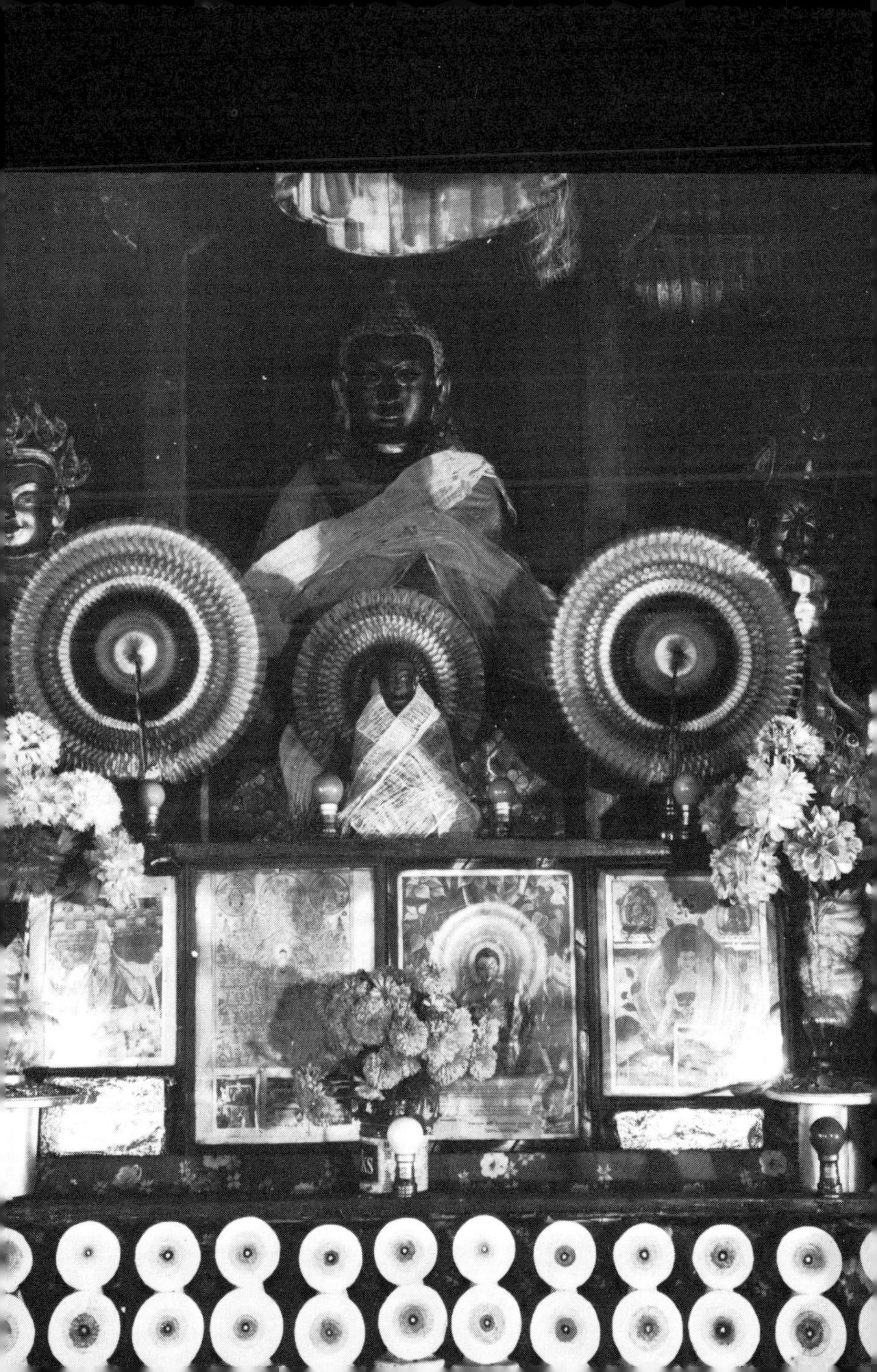

It is, O monks, a realm where there is neither earth, nor water, nor fire, nor wind; it is not the realm of infinite space, nor that of infinite consciousness, nor the realm of nothingness, nor a realm without perception or the absence of perception, nor this world or the other, nor sun or moon. I speak of this realm as neither leaving nor coming nor continuing, death or rebirth, because it has no cause, no progression and no support: it is the end of suffering.

*Udana, VIII,I*

CHAPTER TWO

\* \* \*
\* \*
\*

# THE FOUNDATIONS
# OF BUDDHISM

### SUFFERING

In spite of the limitations of language, the Buddha transmitted to
us a teaching on the plane of relative truth that goes right to the
heart of the greatest human problem – suffering and its ending. In
his teaching, he has deliberately rejected every unrelated question and focused himself entirely on the realization of the goal.

The point of departure of Buddhist thought is a simple asser-
tion: the suffering of man. If the suffering of humanity appears to
all men with a more or less great intensity, the interior and fundamental suffering of each man is only visible to those rare minds
who are free of it. Despite this, man still continues his pursuit of a
utopic happiness.

The Buddha taught: 'It is difficult to shoot arrow after arrow
into a narrow keyhole located a long distance away and not to
miss the target a single time. It is still more difficult to pull and
pierce a fragment of hair split one hundred times with the point of
a piece of hair split in the same way. It is still more difficult to
penetrate the truth that all that exists is suffering.'

'All the earthly goals have only one inevitable end: suffering.
Acquisitions end in dispersions, constructions in destructions,
meetings in separations, birth in death. The body is full of suffering, sensation and perception are full of suffering, activities are full
of suffering, and consciousness is full of suffering.'

### THE FOUR NOBLE TRUTHS

After his Illumination, the Buddha taught the essence of his doctrine in the Deer Park in Benares:

'Lend me your ears, O Monks! The state without death has been found. I will present and reveal the doctrine; in following these precepts, in very little time, in this very life, you will understand the final goal of the holy life, you will realize immortality and remain there.

1. *What is therefore the holy Truth about Evil?*
   Birth is evil, decay is evil, sickness is evil, death is evil. To be joined to what one does not like is to suffer. To be separated from what one likes is to suffer. Not to have what one desires is to suffer. In short, all contact with any one of the five *skandhas* implies suffering.

2. *What is therefore the holy Truth about the origin of Evil?*
   It is this appetite that leads to rebirth, accompanied by pleasure and activity, seeking its pleasure now here and now there; namely, the appetite for sensory experiences, the appetite for perpetuating oneself, and the appetite for extinction.

3. *What is therefore the holy Truth about the cessation of Evil?*
   It is the total cessation of this appetite, the act of keeping oneself from it, of renouncing it, of rejecting it, of delivering oneself from it, and of not attaching oneself to it.

4. *What is therefore the holy Truth about the ways that lead to the cessation of Evil?*
   It is the Eight-fold Path:
   – Correct View,
   – Correct Intention,
   – Correct Action,
   – Correct Speech,
   – Correct Livelihood,
   – Correct Effort
   – Correct Mindfulness,
   – Correct Meditation.


THE SELF AND THE FIVE SKANDHAS


In the conclusion of his first of the Four Noble Truths, the Buddha said: 'All contact with any one of the five *skandhas* implies suffering.'

The illusion of Self is a creation of the union of the *skandhas*, or components of Self. It has nothing to do with the realization of absolute truth. Man and the world are illusions that our ignorance alone makes us see as real. In fact, the Self and the phenomena that appear to us as reality are only a dream, an illusion, an echo, a cloud, a reflection, a shadow, a mirage, an hallucination, as it is written in the *Diamond Sutra*. All contact with any one of the components of Self is a sign of ignorance. The play of these aggregates prevent man from realizing the emptiness of his own fundamentally pure nature. Illumination is the fruit of the transcendence of the illusory contacts with the five *skandhas*, which are:

1. Form or materiality, which includes the elements earth, water, fire, air, as well as every form emanating from them, and these from every physical phenomenon.
2. Sensation and the perceptions of the senses.
3. Concepts and all the notions that form the conscious intellect.
4. The tendencies or potentialities of the mind, the thoughts, the creations of the imagination.
5. Conscious knowledge, discrimination and the fact of being conscious of something.

## THE SELF

In Buddhism, illumination is the realization of the emptiness of Self. The concept of Self that man hopes to save, to unite with the Divine and to enjoy in Heaven, disappears through successive clarifications in Buddhism. The Buddha devoted himself to curtailing this dream in order to point out to man the necessity of standing on his own in order to find the state without suffering, the state where Self no longer exists:

What I see appears and disappears, and because of its impermanence, brings me suffering, and so cannot be myself.

Now, my body, in its wholeness, appears and disappears without end, and due to its impermanence, brings me suffering. Therefore, the body is not my Self.

Now, I see that not only my body but also my mind, all consciousness, appear and disappear endlessly and due to their impermanence bring me suffering. Therefore, neither the body nor the mind is my Self.

Now, all things recognizable in me and around me appear and disappear, and due to their impermanence suffering occurs. Therefore, nothing recognizable is my Self.*

Death is only the end of an illusion. However, Buddha spoke of the creation of an astral body as Paracelsus later did in the West: 'From the physical body of the monk departs another body having a form and consisting of mind, with all the principal and secondary organs, just as when someone pulls a blade of grass from its casing and then thinks: The casing and the blade of grass are two things. However, I pulled the blade from its casing.'

But does this subtle body remain after death? Here is the response of the Buddha:

With the dissolution of the body, all sensations and with them all consciousness in general, will expire just as if, O disciples, there were a shadow cast by a tree, and a man with an axe and a basket came to cut down the tree at the root; after he cuts it at the root, he would have to unearth the roots and pull them out with the finest rootlets; then he would have to cut the trunk into pieces, to split the pieces into fragments. Next he would have to dry them in the wind and sun, burn them and reduce them to ashes; and these ashes he would have to throw into the wind or to scatter into a river of impetuous torrents. Thus, this shadow cast by the tree would be completely destroyed, such as a palm tree torn from the sun would be annihilated and could no longer be reborn in the future. Likewise, at the dissolution of the body, all sensations and all consciousness will also be completely extinguished.[2]

The immortality of Self is only another illusion that causes our blindness and suffering.

Does that mean that death is the end of suffering, and that it is nothingness? This is what you find in most texts refering to Buddhism. However, it is an error. Buddhism is not nihilistic. Only the abandonment of Self allows the realization of the state without suffering.

After his Illumination, in the first sermon at Benares, Buddha said: 'You will realize immortality and remain in it.'

## THE TWELVE HINDRANCES TO LIBERATION

The law that the Buddhists call the law of Karma is the chain of cause and effect. It is in ending these twelve bonds that the meditator attains Illumination. This law rules the entire universe and, as long as Karma exists, birth is the fruit, the sorrow, and the dependent consequence of it.

In order to abolish birth and suffering, the Buddha went back to its origin and through this inverse way, he pointed out the way of liberation.

*The Bonds of Suffering*
On ignorance, Karma depends,
On Karma, consciousness depends,
On consciousness, name and form depend,
On name and form, the sense organs depend,
On the six sense organs, contact depends,
On contact, sensation depends,
On sensation, desire depends,
On desire, attachment depends,
On attachment, existence depends,
On existence, birth depends,
On birth, sorrow, old age, lamentations, misery, regret, despair and death
    depend. Thus, the elements of suffering flow into each other.

*Liberation from Suffering*
Through the dispersion and cessation of ignorance, Karma ceases,
Through the cessation of Karma, consciousness ceases,
Through the cessation of consciousness, name and form cease,
Through the cessation of name and form, the six sense organs cease,
Through the cessation of the six sense organs, contact ceases,
Through the cessation of contact, sensation ceases,
Through the cessation of sensation, desire ceases,
Through the cessation of desire, attachment ceases,
Through the cessation of attachment, existence ceases,
Through the cessation of existence, birth ceases,
Through the cessation of birth, sorrow, old age, lamentations, misery,
    despair, griefs and death cease.
Thus the entire chain of the aggregates of suffering disappears.

## THE DESTRUCTION OF IGNORANCE

Every doctrine of the Buddha, in its practical realization, is attached to the problem of the destruction and cessation of ignorance. With the Noble Path of the Eight-fold Way, the Buddha proposes a precise method of realization: Correct views — Correct speech — Correct action — Correct way of life — Correct effort — Correct will — Correct attention — Correct meditation.

Up above Southern clouds whirl.
Down below a pure river ripples,
Between the two the eagle soars.
Herbs of every species mingle.
Dancing trees wave
The bees sing and *Khor-ro-ro*,
The flowers perfume, and *chi-li-li*,
The birds warble, and *kyru-ru-ru*.

To father, conqueror of the Four Demons
To interpreter Marpa, salute!
Of myself, I have nothing to say.
Of the white lioness of the glaciers, the son I am.
From the womb of the mother, of the triple force completely formed.
All the years of my childhood, in the nest, I have lain.
And in the years of adolescence, the gate of the nest, I have guarded.
But once an adult, on the glaciers I walk.
Even in the storm, I do not vacillate,
Even the great abyss does not make me afraid.

Of myself I have nothing to say.
Of the eagle, the king of birds, the son I am.
From inside the egg, already both my wings were unfolded.
All the years of my childhood in the nest I have lain.
And in the years of adolescence, the gate of the nest, I have guarded.
But once become a full-grown eagle, the summit of heaven I outflew.
In the boundless sky I don't waver,
On the narrow earth I have no fear.

Of myself I have nothing to say.
Of the great fish of the trembling wave, the son I am.
From the womb of the mother, my round golden eyes were formed.
All the years of my childhood, in the nest, I have lain.
And in the years of my adolescence always at the shoal's head, I swam.
Finally adult and a great fish, all around the ocean I swim.
In the ground swell, I don't waver,
Fishing nets do not frighten me.

Of myself I have nothing to say.
Of the guru's oral teaching, the son I am.
From the womb of the mother, faith in myself was already born.
From the years of my childhood, into the religious life, I entered.
And the years of adolescence I spent studying the doctrine.
Finally adult and a great meditator, the mountain hermitages I haunt.
Faced with demons I don't waver,
Their phantasmagoria I do not fear.

## Correct Views and Correct Speech

Correct views are the comprehension of the Four Noble Truths taught by the Buddha. In fact, the Buddha always avoided defining to his disciples the views that he considered as 'right,' for they comprised the totality of his doctrine, including the transcendence of dualistic concepts. Correct views are related to the first part of the doctrine, which belongs to the world of form by its very expression. The other part goes beyond all concepts and therefore cannot be the object of any view.

On this subject, it is important to emphasize that the Buddha never sought an adherence to his doctrine based on faith. On the contrary, he always emphasized that an adhesion to his doctrine could only be based on the realization of its teaching. Therefore, the correct views do not concern a belief but a total transformation of the being in its depths.

Correct speech is the abstention of speech each time the intention is not elevated. The great master Chih-chi of T'ien-t'ai in his treatise, *Dhyana for Novices*,[3] gives a commentary of correct speech: 'One must remember that in speaking one awakens good or bad sensations, which irritate and trouble the mind. Also, it is necessary to remember that the *personality* that speaks has no visible appearance and that it is as vain as all the perturbations of the mind that depend on the act of speaking.'

## Correct Action and Correct Way of Life

Correct action is the abstention from every action that is not undertaken in an elevated way. As is true for speech, it is essential to realize in action the emptiness of the acting principle. Action disturbs the mind; it is empty.

Correct way of life must be understood as a way of living that is in accord with spiritual research and that carries prejudice to no one.

## Correct Effort and Correct Will

Correct effort and will consist in the most intensive determination to attain the state without suffering. According to Scriptures, there are four kinds of efforts.

1. *Effort in order to avoid.* To strive to prevent false and unhealthy ideas from penetrating into one's mind, and to strive not to commit bad acts that one has not yet committed.

2. *Effort in order to dominate.* To strive to annihilate the harmful tendencies that one feels in oneself and not to allow them to take root. To combat lust, anger, and illusion by vanquishing and rejecting them. There are five ways of overcoming harmful thoughts: to oppose a healthy idea to the harmful one; to consider the evil effects of the harmful idea and not to give any attention to it; to analyze it; to uncover the elements that constitute it and the causes that have engendered it; to fortify oneself with a strong will and to oppose it fiercely.

3. *Effort in order to acquire.* To strive to awaken in oneself all the healthy tendencies that one does not yet possess. Acquire the necessary qualities in order to arrive at knowledge, namely: attention, penetration, energy, interest, tranquillity, mental stability and concentration.

4. *Effort in order to maintain.* To strive to conserve the healthy notions and tendencies that one possesses, not to allow oneself to weaken, to work to develop them and to lead them to their perfection.

## Correct Attention

Attention is one of the most important phases of realization if one wants to attain significant spiritual progress. In his teaching, Buddha insisted strongly on the benefits of attention, which is the gate of access to meditation. It is the preparation and the foundation because without it no contemplative practice can bear its fruits. Numerous techniques have been elaborated in order to develop it, to conserve it and to transcend it. It consists in the observation and mastery of all that occurs in us on the physical plane as well as on the mental plane. It consists equally in being totally aware of what surrounds us and of perceiving the profound significance of things as well as movements. This effort of observation and knowledge is divided into four parts:

1. The observation of the body.
2. The observation of sensations.
3. The observation of thought.

4. The observation of internal phenomena and of the workings
   of the mind.

We will examine these different techniques in detail in the
fourth chapter, which is devoted to Hinayana, the Buddhism of
Origins.

## CORRECT MEDITATION

Correct meditation (*jhana* in Pali and *dhyana* in Sanskrit can both
be translated equally by concentration) is the last path of the
Noble Eight-fold Path. Through it the Buddhist attains the state
without death, Illumination, Nirvana. The meditator, having dis-
ciplined his body and mind by attention, obtains the ultimate liberation through the practice of meditation. The techniques of
meditation vary according to the different schools, and we will
describe in detail those that are related to Hinayana Buddhism, to
Mahayana, to Vajrayana, to Ch'an or Zen, and finally in the last part,
to Taoism.

Meditation, for Buddhists and Taoists, is the interior revolution
that allows one to experience and realize the emptiness of the ego
as well as of phenomena by a succession of insights that dissolve
the world of distinct entities. Every duality and concept are then
transcended, and the disciple bathes in the pure state of mind, free
from every form. He is neither prisoner of being nor of non-being.
It is the outcome of the Buddha's teaching. It is that which he himself named Nirvana.

## NIRVANA

'It is, O Monks, a domain where there is neither earth, nor water,
nor fire, nor wind, nor the infinite domain of space, nor the infinite
domain of consciousness, nor the domain of nothingness, nor the
domain without perceptions or the absence of perceptions, nor
this world or the other world, nor sun or moon. This domain, I
name neither going, nor coming, nor enduring, neither deceased,
nor reborn because it is without foundation, progression and support: it is the end of suffering.'

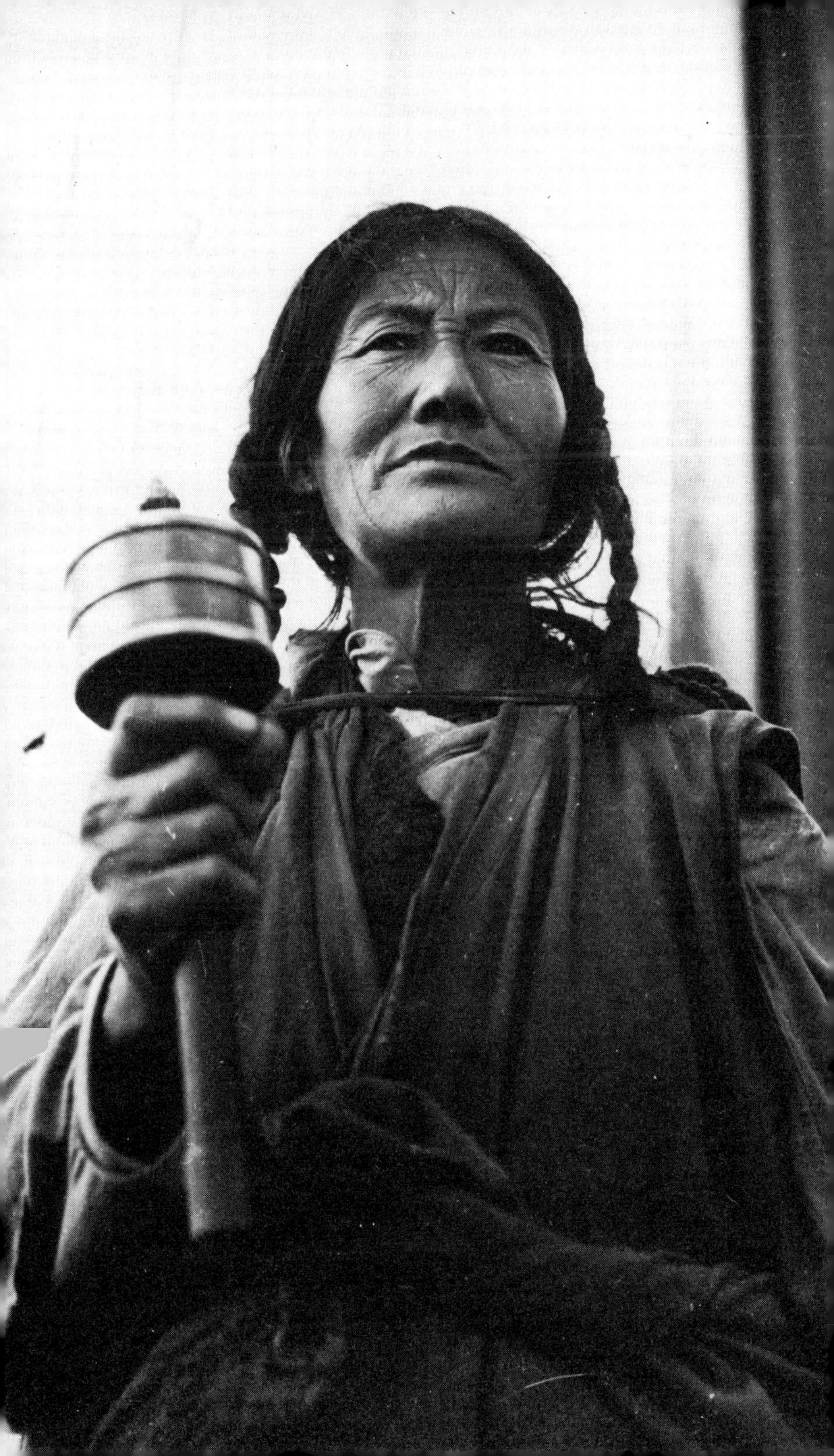

Truly, Brothers, all that a compassionate, sympathetic and loving Master owes to his disciples, I have given to you.

Here, the shade of the forests calls you; further on, the vast solitude. Dedicate yourselves, O Brothers, to Meditation so that laziness does not envelop you and so that you will not regret it later on.

Keep this for your commandment. Everything is impermanent. Through your intensity, attain your goal.

*Anguttura Nikaya*

\* \* \*
\* \*
\*

## CHAPTER THREE

# PREPARATION FOR MEDITATION

## THE STUDY OF THE WAY AND THE CLEAR COMPREHENSION

A thorough study of the different paths of the Way and a clear understanding of the principles of Buddhism such as they are revealed in the second chapter are necessary in order to realize the teaching through meditation. From this foundation, a group of practices and divergent techniques are developed that must be realized profoundly. It is only after this study that one can be oriented toward the knowledge of cause and can avoid stumbling during the first attempts at practice. It is important for one not to attempt to begin practices unattainable for beginners. The only guarantee of future progress is to begin with the most simple exercises.

*The Search for the Master.* Because of incomplete, badly chosen, and superficial readings, jumbled fictions, scholastic imaginations and arid orientalists, those who aspire to realize a fundamental experience from meditation often mistakenly engage themselves in practical exercises, either alone, or under the guidance of masters who are only, in fact, gymnastic teachers. This approach, so frequent in Western countries, can provoke serious psychic disorders and even lead to mental illness. Certain unbridled mental forces, when they are not totally controlled, provoke a veritable mental explosion and leave the yoga apprentices in a form of insanity from which they sometimes never recover.

The presence of a master is indispensable for all thorough study. He knows all the subtleties of the road that will be traversed by the disciple, and can not only guide him but can also prevent him from losing his way in numerous difficulties. In addition, through the transfer of a psychic force, the master can from the start give the disciple an extraordinary energy that permits him to experience a kind of necessary orbital propulsion. This sudden launching is so powerful that it equips him with a form of realization at the outset, which he will later have to repeat on his own. Here one gets a glimpse of the goal, which is not theoretical but has been experienced through a brief Illumination provoked by the master in the course of the initiation. All the schools recognize the importance of a master, but each looks at it from a different angle. The master alone can render to his disciple the accessible, clear, luminous way, by giving to him not *a* method but *the* method that agrees with his personality. At the beginning, as well as at the end, the master will always be there in order to provide light and open new and unending horizons.

## THE REFUGE

When the disciple has understood the basic teachings and has found a master, he takes triple refuge in the Buddha, the Dharma and the Sangha: the instructor, the doctrine and the community of monks.

'My humblest respect to the Lord, the Emancipator and the Illumined! May I receive the triple refuge and the five precepts. I take refuge in the Buddha, I take refuge in the Dharma, I take refuge in the Sangha.'

Each of these injunctions is repeated three times. They mark the entrance of the disciple into the field of Buddhism and constitute a kind of baptism. The refuge is a conscious act, a choice one makes after an examination of the doctrine; it is certainly neither a question of dogma nor of faith; it is simply an adherence to a method that the disciple thinks is capable of leading to liberation.

## THE FIVE PRECEPTS

The masters of all the schools of Buddhism unceasingly repeat that no true progress can be made in the way of meditation without the observation of five fundamental precepts:

1. No killing.
2. No stealing.
3. No lying.

4. No committing of sexual impurity.
5. Abstaining from every drug or intoxicating substance.

Westerners, for whom the existence of precepts is often very bothersome, manage to give them a secondary importance. But in fact, they are the only logical base of every accomplishment.

## THE TEN PARAMITA

After a period of preliminary practice and strict observation of the five precepts, the Master also asks the disciple to observe the Ten Paramita, without which one cannot go beyond the rudiments of meditation. They are:

1. Charity
2. Morality
3. Renunciation
4. Energy
5. Courage
6. Truth
7. Intensive resolution
8. Compassion
9. Equanimity
10. Wisdom

All these virtues are tied to each other, and the development of each of them assists in making possible a step-by-step progress. However, the third Paramita can be considered the foundation stone not only of the other virtues but also of meditation.

## THE RENUNCIATION

Renunciation can be the greatest stumbling block on the way to meditation. Its realization is an extremely important step in the disciple's life. The Buddha, as Jesus and nearly all the great teachers, made it the primary virtue that allows one to enter easily into the contemplative life and to arrive quickly at the realization of the teaching. The greater the renunciation, the faster the progress.

The renunciation is the second obstacle that Westerners prefer

to forget in the study and practice of Buddhism. What Tantric
writings could be read on a deep level as claiming that virtue and
renunciation are only an adornment of the principle destined for
ordinary men, of which we, of course, are not a part? Such
attitudes are intellectual defences which are not anchored in the
depths of being. Everyone who is honest with himself knows that
without sacrifices and efforts no method will permit the blossoming of concentration and the interior vision.

Renunciation is all the more difficult to practice because the
masters of Buddhism have described in great detail the meaning
that they give to this term and to its different applications.

First of all, it is necessary to renounce the world; namely, physical and mental contacts with the world. In order to do this, it is
necessary to abandon every intellectual, affective, spiritual,
economic and social relationship with the world. The world must
be abandoned physically and spiritually. One must forget its culture and no longer utilize the ways that have been taught. This is
one of the greatest difficulties. The mind must be emptied of the
material that clutters it; for only an empty mind can be penetrated
by Light. It is also necessary to free the mind of projections,
dreams and remembrances, these can block the disciple's progress. Finally, it is necessary to suspend the superficial activity of
discriminating that conditions our everyday life.

'The Buddha attained total deliverance by the complete rejection of all opinions and conjectures.' It is also necessary to
renounce bodily desire and sensual satisfaction, as they prevent
the growth of concentration.

The disciple does not do all this in order to immerse himself in
imaginings of another type. He must renounce every thought of
the goal and must not imagine the successive levels of his asceticism. In not reaching his goal, the meditator risks experiencing
only the pale reflection of his mental formations, becoming victim
to a simple phenomenon of auto-suggestion. The experience of
meditation allows a release from the universe of words, images
and mental formations; therefore, every activity of mind can only
prevent this process.

When Sariputra questioned the Buddha on the way of transcendent knowledge, the latter responded:

'Sariputra, the Bodhisattva is on the way to knowledge when he
doesn't abandon himself to his imaginings, when he imagines
neither body, nor word, nor mind, nor any of the six excellent vir-

tues (charity, morality, patience, concentration, meditation, wisdom) nor doctrine; and then, imagining nothing, he takes nothing and rejects nothing.

'He has neither the covetousness of the eye and its object, nor the covetousness of the ear and sound, nor the covetousness of the nose and scent, nor the covetousness of the tongue and taste, nor the covetousness of the body and touch, nor the covetousness of the mind and mental formations. He is free from the covetousness of the domain of earth, of water, of fire, and the wind of space and consciousness.'

This total renunciation seems beyond the reach of man and can discourage every sincere aspirant. The Buddha, contrary to many others, has not established a goal nor stated a rule without giving at the same time a very precise method that permits its realization. These techniques are explained in detail in the following chapters.

### SOLITUDE AND PLACES OF MEDITATION

The Tibetan Masters recommend remaining in solitude until one has achieved the proper discipline of mind and body, after which it is possible to live in the community with the other monks without it becoming a hindrance to spiritual development. However, they do not specify the duration of this period of solitude, which depends on the possibilities of the individual. The texts speak of an average duration of twelve continuous years.

Come, O Monks! Remain in a secluded place; in a forest, under a tree, on a hill, in a cave, a mountain grotto, in a cemetery, in a jungle bush, an open place, or in a shelter of straw in the fields. The monk remains in such secluded places, and after the meal, having collected his alms, he sits down cross-legged, keeping his body erect and his attention vigilant. Having abandoned covetousness concerning the world, he remains with his heart free of covetousness; he strips his mind of covetousness. Having abandoned the stain of hatred concerning the world, he remains with a heart free of hatred, loving and compassionate to all living beings. He strips his mind of the stain of hatred. Having abandoned numbness and dullness, he remains with a heart free of numbness and dullness, in the contemplation of Light, attentive and clearly perceptive; he strips his mind of numbness and dullness. Having abandoned agitation and anxiety, he remains with the heart not agitated, the mind in peace; he strips his mind of agitation and anxiety. Having abandoned doubt, he has left incertitude behind him and he is no longer uncertain about wholesome things; he strips his mind of doubt.[1]

To the places of meditation cited by the Buddha, one can add river banks, springs, deserts, and high summits. It is important to choose a place that is suitable climatically and that is not totally contrary to one's normal environment. A very abrupt change would prevent concentration and well-being.

The masters recommend as well not to indulge in wandering from place to place, which would disturb the mind. The perfect place does not exist, but it creates itself slowly through the spiritual vibrations released by the disciple in the course of his meditations. The places frequented by a number of ascetics are equally very beneficial since the energies accumulate, and then each benefits from the vibrations of others. This phenomenon is particularly evident in certain regions of the Himalayas.

## THE HERMITAGE

There are numerous conditions that enter into play at the time a choice is made in regard to a hermitage. Certain monks are as specialized in the subtle art of choosing a hermitage as others are in exorcism or the teaching of meditation. Contacted by the aspirants, they stroll through isolated places like water-diviners with their senses and intuition wide awake. Entire works are devoted to the ideal conditions, but their main points can be summarized here:

— Food must be available, either through residents who take the meditator into their care and thus permit him to remain in his hermitage (as is most often done); or at a nearby village (at least 2 miles from the hermitage), where the ascetic can go to beg for his food; or else, through the cultivation of the bare necessities by the meditator himself. Finally, but much more rarely, the knowledge of wild plants allows certain ascetics to remain in total solitude in the heart of the forest or on inaccessible mountain heights. Sometimes several ascetics gather in small, isolated villages and organize in order to provide for themselves.

— The place should be remote from every built-up area and from every human creation that could by its noise, odors, view or subtle vibrations, disturb the ascetic in his practices.

— The place should be healthy, and one must be able to obtain care in case of serious illness.

— The divinatory aspects of the places should be favorable.

— The hermitage should be at the side of a mountain and, if possible, overlook a body of water, lake, pond or river. When there is no water, it should overlook a field, a valley, or some hills, and the limits of the horizon should be enclosed by a high mountain chain.

— The rising and setting of the sun as well as its journey across the sky should be visible from the hermitage.

— The spirits of the place should be favorable to the ascetic, and if he senses a hostile presence, he should find another place to build his hermitage.

— The Master is the most qualified person to choose the place of retreat for his disciple. By taking into account his personality, individual characteristics and the goal of meditation to which he has initiated his student, the Master will know instinctively what is the most profitable place for harmonious development.

There are different types of hermitages. They depends upon the construction of the place and the anticipated duration of seclusion.

— A tree is the simplest, most classic shelter. Its foliage provides protection from excessive light and bad weather conditions, and its trunk provides a place to lean on. It is a powerful vehicle of beneficial vibrations and fluids. It was under a tree that the Buddha and numerous ascetics attained Illumination.

– An opening in the earth exposed to the sun forms a simple dwelling that needs to be protected only by some branches. This system was much used not only in the Orient, but equally in the West. A great number of these holes exist, notably in Ireland on the Islands of Aran. Here, as well, the subtle telluric vibrations are an important source of energy for the ascetic.

– Grottoes are the most preferred places. The temperature is stable, cool in summer and mild in winter. A special silence, favorable to long ecstasies, exists in both grottoes and caves. Tilopa, Milarepa, and a great number of other sages lived in them for many years. However, only those who possess a great physical and spiritual force can remain in a grotto. The atmosphere is not healthy and can cause skin diseases, among other things. What is more, this complete solitude sometimes provokes a certain imbalance in those who do not possess sufficient yogic experience.

– Wooden, earthen or stone huts occur widely in forests and on mountains. Their construction varies according to its location. In general, they are very suitable and are recommended for beginners.

– Flat-roofed cottages are more elaborate. You see them in countries where Tibetan culture is dominant. Often constructed above a stream, they are totally shut off from the outside world. The ascetic remains walled in total seclusion, which rarely lasts less than twelve years and often is prolonged until death. Sometimes there are two floors; the terrace of the roof is surrounded by a wall in order to conceal the meditator, who sees only the heavens above his head when he is relaxing. His food is sent to him only through a trap-door. In his book, *The Way of the White Clouds*,[2] Anagarika Govinda gives a description of these places: 'Each of these cells was conceived in order to permit its resident to have air, water, and sun, to do physical exercise and also to contemplate the infinite spaces, the immensity of heaven, its celestial bodies, the movements of its clouds and the changes of season. These hermitages were not designed to be places of torture or penitence, but oases of peace and meditation that nothing would disturb. Far from resembling tombs, they are supposed to be waiting rooms of Happiness, as their name indicates. Their general impression gave me an ardent desire to retire one day to one of

these cells for a long period of introspection and uninterrupted
sadhana. . . . The schedule of the *gom-chen* was perfectly regulated and filled by study, worship, and meditation, interspersed
with physical exercises, meals, manual labor required for the preparation of the meals, grooming and the general upkeep of the
cell.'

Finally, near the monasteries in which the great masters of
meditation reside, there are square or rectangular buildings
where the cells surround and enclose a court reserved for physical exercise. In general, these cells are tiny – about a yard per side
– and the meditators live in them in time periods of three (three
years, three months, three days), which can be repeated as the
master and disciple think it necessary. The ascetics sleep a few
hours each night, remaining outside in the lotus position. In general, there is no opening to the outside world, and no one can
enter without having received the corresponding initiation. The
advantages of this system are, on one hand, the concentration of
beneficial fluids, and on the other hand, the nearness of the master, who can guide the disciple each time that it is necessary. Few
Westerners have ever submitted to such a harsh discipline.

## THE CONDITION OF RETREAT

For many Westerners, the ascetic's choice of withdrawing into
retreat until the time of Illumination seems to be an egotistical act,
devoid of concern for the community. The retreat from the world
is often even viewed as a personal insult to those who live in a
troubled milieu. In the Orient, on the contrary, one who retires
from the world enjoys a high level of respect because everyone
knows to what degree the world and its illusions cling to man, the
difficulty of renouncing them and the grandeur and inner force
that it implies. The life of an ascetic is seen not as an egotistical act,
but rather as an act of courage that prevents the world from completely crumbling. What causes these different outlooks? In the
Orient, each human being is considered to diffuse about him an
energy that is the reflection of his mind. These waves accumulate,
collide and contend with each other, and the varying degrees of
density of the beneficial and evil waves influence the behavior of
those who are in their field of concentration. Thus, we bathe in an
ocean of waves produced by all mankind, and according to the

places and persons with whom we have contact, our own mind becomes darkened or enlightened. By withdrawing from the world the sage produces states of ecstasy whose powerful waves benefit those who approach him and all those with receptive sensitivities. The more ascetics and sages there are, the more the currents that are spread throughout the world will be powerful and beneficial. The more evil and darkness spread throughout the earth, the more will their influence be pervasive, and the more will the world approach total chaos. There is nothing mysterious about it, and each can experience it in his daily life. Certain beings awaken light in us and others darkness.

The misunderstanding of this constant state of influence is one of the causes of the Western misunderstanding of Oriental practices. The other reason is less evident and is related to certain concepts of Buddhist doctrine. Man suffers because he is tied to the world of phenomena. The ascetic is detached from illusion, and in the heart of his retreat he penetrates the reality of the world that he alone can know. Those who think they are living in the world only live in appearances of which they are the unconscious instruments. They can help no one, and each of their attempts is like the blind leading the blind. The ascetic departs from appearances and, in the knowledge of the emptiness of all phenomena, he allows the world to penetrate his being through an act of perfect love and wisdom. Only the enlightened can understand in depth the great inherent suffering in the human condition and save those who come to him. This state of enlightenment is not a utopia, nor a thing that occurs after death, but an immediate action that must be undertaken alone. The fruits of this luminious revolution are known from the very beginning. It has nothing to do with having faith, and it is enough to begin with a body and a mind. The task is arduous, but it is realizable in all stages and at all levels immediately. As the Buddha said, 'Be your own refuge.'

It is difficult to form a precise idea of the life of the recluse. It is a life of courage, energy and determination, but it is not a condemned life nor one of isolation. One enormous step must be taken: renunciation. This is the step that separates so many of us from realization. It is more pleasant to think about the solitude and ecstasy. But to abandon everything, to strip away everything, materially as well as in thought: who can do it and who wants to do it? Only a few individuals. One can make a start, detach oneself gradually from things, or at least think that one is. . . Yet all those who have done it say that the mind is filled with Light as soon as one accomplishes the act of renunciation. It begins immediately, and it is so effective that it is rare for someone to go backwards after this initial step.

The first fruits of liberation appear spontaneously. Then begins the retreat, the life of the recluse. The mind and body are relieved of matter and freedom appears. But it will be necessary to work at it day after day. Alexandra David–Neel, who experienced this way of life, gives a description of it in *Mystics and Magicians of Tibet:*[3]

Their period of retreat, however long it may last, is not spent in inaction. The hours are lost track of . . . and are filled with the systematic toil of spiritual training, research into certain kinds of occult knowledge, or better still, meditation on philosophical problems. Thus, involved in their investigations and their introspections, which often interest them deeply, these men are far from being idle and are hardly aware of their isolation.

Even at the beginning of their retreat, I have never heard a single recluse say that he had suffered from lack of human companionship. Generally, those who have tasted this existence can never go back to living in populated areas and resume social relationships. . . . There is a feeling of almost voluptuous sweetness when one closes the gate of his *tshamkhang*, or else, when from the top of his hermitage, he watches the first snow fall in the valley, while thinking that during the ensuing months it is going to seal him off from everything.

DIET

The Buddha himself, after seven years of fasting, ascetic practices and austerities, cautioned his disciples against excessive severities and recommended the middle way situated between the two extremes. An excessively rich and heavy diet is a source of problems, sickness, mental apathy and drowsiness. It is a serious obstacle to meditation. On the other hand, an excessively meager diet deteriorates the body and ends by attacking the nerve centers, which atrophy and become irritated at the least contact. The discomforts produced by hunger disturb cerebral activity and weaken determination. Neither of these two ways can give the disciple the great equilibrium and the psychic and physical strength necessary for his development. According to a sutra:

'The resolution to attain Illumination comes with the strength of the body. Eating and drinking must be controlled. It is neces-

It was in the monastery of Khempo Kalo Rinpoche, at Sonada, a half hour by jeep from Darjeeling, that I was able day after day to integrate myself in the life of the Tibetan Kagyupa Monastery and to see how a great Lama lived and taught. This great Lama's line and tradition goes back to Milarepa in an unbroken descent.

From the upper level of the temple where I lived, every morning at three o'clock I heard the chants of the monks who remained secluded in a one-meter-square cell, for triple time periods lasting up to twelve years. At night, the shadows of the faces of those whose long meditation plunged them deep into emptiness were projected on a screen by the glimmer of an oil lamp. These men chanted mantras and read the sutras; the music of their low rough voices mixed with the sounds of small bells.

No one was allowed to enter the square space that the cells formed around a few dozen meters of land. Here the meditators relaxed from the seated position that they kept night and day taking only a few steps at the time of two allowed breaks.

Later, the chants slipped into the silence of contemplation until nine o'clock in the evening. At six o'clock in the morning, the other monks rose to read the sutras. In spite of the cold, damp winter, the young monks sat bundled up in the grass chanting the Sacred Texts for at least two hours in a single strong, rhythmic voice. Around eight o'clock, the monastery came alive.

Beyond the confines of the section reserved for continuous meditation, there is no place more alive than a Tibetan monastery. In the building

where dining takes place, there are a few blackened pots, an earthen fire place and pieces of meat curing naturally in the smoke as a woman prepares oatmeal in large cauldrons. This is the daily food of the monks, accompanied by tea that is churned for a long time with salt and yak butter. Tsampa, a barley flour, is the only variation in the meals; mixed with tea, it forms a very energetic thick cereal.

For many years Tchuga, who is close to Khempo Kalo Rinpoche, has assured by her presence the perfect equilibrium of a world entirely dedicated to the realization of the Lama's teaching. She serves as a kind of mother to each of the monks, and her extraordinary presence helps make Sonada a place of joy and harmony.

After a bowl of tsampa Kalo Rinpoche gives himself completely to the

meditation center. Day after day, he guides the best of his disciples toward Illumination.

As he leaves, he walks into several buildings of the monastery and talks to the monks about their work. One repairs the roof of the temple, another does the washing, others repair the building or fashion the divinities that will be set into the mandala that is in progress. Some monks have left at least an hour ago in order to gather tea on nearby hills. A young monk about ten years old learns to play the Tibetan horn. In front of him, figured musical notations are displayed in an open book.

The monastic tailor prepares some fur jackets for the winter cold. The monastery is not heated. From the day of my initiation, each morning, I spend an hour following the teachings of Kalo Rinpoche. I begin to learn

a little Tibetan. In the afternoon, visitors come from all parts of India. Kalo Rinpoche is there, seated in his cell, available to everyone and for anything. I sat at his side each day with a few monks and listened to stories of travelers that were partially translated for me. The bursts of laughter continued almost until evening. Tibetans love funny stories. Sometimes, an ascetic comes down from the snowy solitude of the Himalayas to receive instruction. Some Tibetans come to ask advice. All questions are treated with the same interest. Thus, life unfolds under all its aspects from the most serious to the most comic. Each visitor brings an offering – an orange, a ball of thread, a tea biscuit, or a piece of fabric.

Towards the end of the afternoon, everyone meets inside the temple. Chants, music and lectures on the sutras. The ceremony lasts two hours.

The extraordinary drone of the music moves everyone towards concentration. The whole being floats on a magnificent sonorous wave that makes every fiber vibrate.

In the evening, assembled around Rinpoche, we speak of the day's ending and tomorrow's projects. Later, nothing remains but silence, the starry sky and the whiteness of the stupa that stands out against the background of the frozen night.

sary to keep the mind peaceful and avoid troubling thoughts. When the mind is calm, one finds a great satisfaction in the practice of meditation. Such are the teachings of all the Buddhas.'

## SLEEP

Everything in the life of the meditator must be perfectly regulated. Sleep is very important in the life of the aspirant. Listlessness and indolence are great enemies of spiritual realization. In this case also, it is advisable to follow the middle way taught by the Buddha. Too much sleep clouds the mind and encourages states of doubt and depression. After awakening, it is very important not to fall into a state of prolonged drowsiness. Too little sleep is detrimental to a good equilibrium of mind and body. The meditator must set the exact time of sleep necessary for him to feel at ease, and he must make it a habit to fall asleep and wake up at the same time every day.

During meditation, drowsiness is one of the great enemies of realization, and all the masters, in all the schools, have provided numerous techniques to remedy it. Beginners, after having relaxed the body during the first stage of meditation, are in such a state of calmness that they fall asleep. Then they mistake their sleep for a meditative state and reimmerse themselves in it automatically. Fortunately, there are numerous remedies; let us mention, among others, walking accompanied by concentration, changing the respiratory rhythm, changing place or subject of concentration, concentrating on light, performing yoga exercises and reciting sacred formulas.

## PHYSICAL AND MENTAL CALM

In his discussion on meditation, the Great Master Chih-chi of T'ien-t'ai[4] said 'that it is necessary to establish a gradual progression from a state of physical activity to a state of mental tranquillity. Respiration must become smooth and quiet, and the stream of mental activity must subside and become unperceived. Then one must regulate and adjust the activities of the mind in the same way that one regulates the body up to the point where tranquillity and peace are established.'

This preparation is the springboard to more elaborate activities, which by different procedures of progressive self-effacement, permit the meditator to reach emptiness.

The Tibetans equally recommend the cessation of all activities. For this they recommend a rather simple exercise. Carried to perfection, it can by itself lead to one of the four contemplations without form described in the following chapter, or even to all four contemplations. It is quite obvious that the subject of this passage on meditation is not ordained merely to be *formulated* inside but to be *realized* by the disciple in the silence of mind:

I let go, I turn aside, I put down all agreeable or painful memories relating to what I have done or would have wanted to do in the past, relating to all the episodes of my past activity. I let go, I put down what I have been or would have wished to be in the past. I let go, I put down the impressions that I have felt, I discharge and strip myself of them.

I let go, I put down all that preoccupies me now, all that relates to my present activity and to that which would be able to touch me in the activity of other people: my ambitions, my fears, everything that my interest carries me towards.

I let go, I put down all cares concerning the future, the projects of spiritual or material order: desire for success, fears of failures whatever they may be, all certainties, all doubts as to what I will be or to what will happen to me tomorrow or in the distant future[5].


## FOR THE WESTERNERS


The attitude of the Westerners regarding the ascetic splendors of the Orient most often seems to be reduced only to intellectual admiration. The pitfalls of civilization, of thought, of religion and of philosophy that have conditioned our minds seem to separate us from every serious ascetic practice. Can these things be practiced half way? The farther one is from being totally involved, the greater the difficulties and the slower the progress. Many try, but nearly all give up because of the slowness of their progress. To accomodate the Westerners, some have tried to adapt the methods of meditation to their culture. It has even come to the point of speaking of 'Christian Zen.'. . . Need the total absurdity of such systems be emphasized? They can only lead to failure if not to serious physical and psychic disorders. Jung himself examined more than one case of this type, and it is on good grounds that he

wrote in his commentary on *The Tibetan Book of the Great Liberation*:

> If the European could go into himself and live as an Oriental with all the
> social, moral, intellectual and aesthetic obligations that go along with it,
> he could probably benefit from these teachings. But you cannot be a good
> Christian, in your faith, your morality, or your intellectual makeup and
> practice yoga at the same time. . . . If it is possible for you to seat your-
> self on gazelle skin under a bo tree or in a gompa's cell for the rest of your
> life without ever being troubled by politics or the fall of your finances,
> then I would consider your case. But yoga in Mayfair, or on Fifth Avenue,
> or in any other place with a telephone is a spiritual fiction.[6]

Is it therefore necessary to give up hope of grasping the contemplative way from any other perspective than that of intellectual understanding? Giving up would be preferrable if there is no
strong determination as a foundation. Otherwise, there are several provisional and preparatory solutions.

The best consists in freeing oneself from the world in a tempor-
ary manner, as long as possible (three months is considered the
minimum), and in having, most importantly, a good knowledge of
Oriental philosophy and spirituality. In addition, you must have
enough money to provide for your needs during the whole
period. For the past few years, with charters and travel at reduced
prices, it has been possible to reach the Orient at reasonable cost.
Once you are there, sixty dollars a month is enough to cover
expenses in most countries. Then, there is the problem of finding
a master. It is a question of luck and determination. Northern
India, the Himalayas, Sri Lanka and Thailand are the places that
offer the best chances of success. There are many monasteries for
the three vehicles, Hinayana, Mahayana and Vajrayana. Meditation
isn't practiced everywhere. Certain monasteries are specialized
and their Great Masters are surrounded by numerous disciples. It
is in these places that you will have the best chance of receiving
serious teaching since it is addressed primarily to monks who
have decided to dedicate their lives to these practices. More
importantly, the atmosphere is favorable right from the beginning. To find a master that is by himself is much more difficult, and
it requires previous experience in order to judge his qualities.
Avoid, in whatever measure possible, the places where there are
already a large number of Westerners. These places are often filled
with an atmosphere of childish competition and jealousy that is
not suited to the desired goal. Equally avoid Westerners who have

become monks. They have an unfortunate tendency of overestimating their qualities, and those who pass themselves off as masters are really beginners. You might as well stay in Europe where the same beginners open ashrams and centers of meditation. The most important thing is to choose a place, a master and a method and remain with them. It is the only way to make rapid progress. Having done that, you must not doubt the capacities of your master and must practice with strength and determination. An atmosphere in which everyone is pursuing the same goal is a very great help. The body grows calm, the mind finds a more natural rhythm and progress is felt day by day.

When you first get there, despite the amount of effort you put into your first attempts, for a while you will have the feeling that you are always starting again from zero. The presence of all the problems of daily life will accentuate this impression, and you risk living in the memories of the Light rather than in the Light. However, if your attitude about everyday life is transformed, if your attachment diminishes, you should persevere; you may succeed. On the other hand, if your practices do not modify your natural tendency, then failure is imminent.

### THE WESTERN HERMITAGE

At home it is often impossible to construct a hermitage unless you live outside the city. For those who live in cities, the only solution is a room in an apartment, or still more simply, a corner of a room set up for this purpose. A tiny room where the air can circulate is ideal. Large rooms are not advisable because the energies produced are scattered and the concentration takes more time to develop. No one must be allowed to enter the room that you have chosen, and you must only use it for your meditations. Every outside activity, every thought relative to the world of phenomena will soil the atmosphere. Burn incense there before beginning your meditation, and place in front of you an image of your master, the Buddha or a Great Sage. In order to meditate at ease, clothing which does not pressure the body or hinder posture in any way is necessary. A robe is ideal.

Finally, there remain a few material conditions that are necessary to observe because there are already enough obstacles.

No heating, it numbs the mind.

A free circulation of air.

A seat for meditation, its cushion made of *natural* material. Plastics and synthetic foams isolate the radiations.

Be as near as possible to the earth. Every separation or material interference acts as a screen and deprives you of the energies indispensable to the attainment of a good meditation. As soon as the opportunity presents itself, leave the city and meditate in the open air, in peaceful places, near ponds or rivers, in forests or on mountains.

Practicing with regularity provides the greatest opportunity for success. If possible, as soon as longer periods become available, (weekends or vacations) practice continuously in complete isolation away from the city. These are the periods that will be most precious and will permit you to find the states ordinarily experienced in the presence of a master.

The power of thought, in spite of great distance, can join you to a master, after a certain stage, and if you have access to him, his waves of blessing will penetrate you wherever you may be.

One last point: you must avoid speaking of the practices that you carry out; avoid telling others the experiences that you know; the contact of words soils and limits them.

*Chatral Rinpoche in his monastery of Ghoom near Darjeeling, India. Of the Kagyupa order, he continues the tradition of the school of Milarepa.*

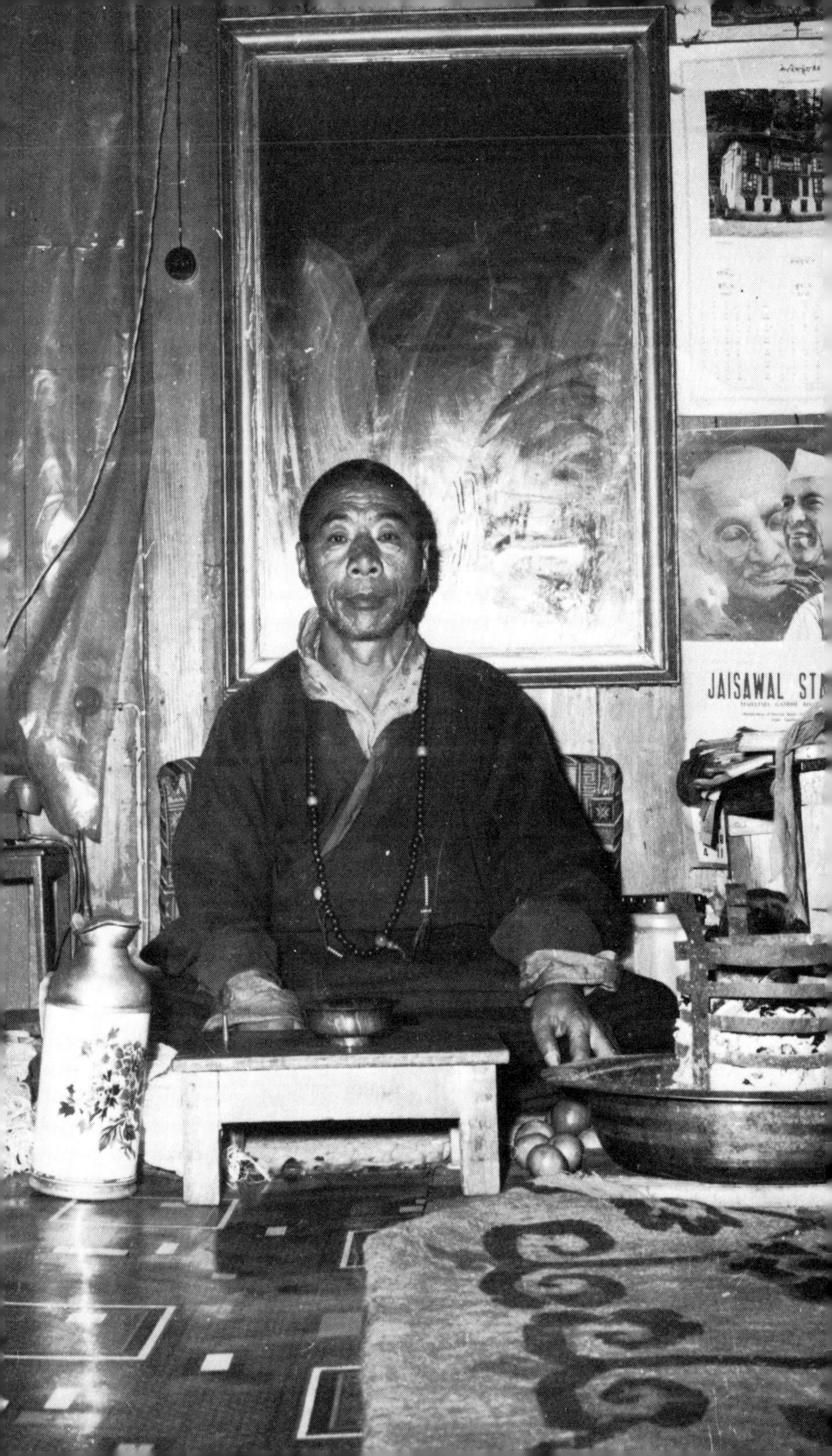
JAISAWAL STA

One day the Venerable One was at Uruvela, on the bank of the Nairanjana River, under the Goat-herds' fig tree, and while he was alone, the following thought came to him: the only road to purify beings, to overcome sadness and sorrow, to destroy suffering and affliction, to reach the true path, to realize Nirvana, is the four establishments of mindfulness.

It has been demonstrated infallibly that the four establishments of mindfulness are the only way the Buddhas have followed. Always keep them!

*Nagarjuna*

*   *   *

*   *

*

## CHAPTER FOUR

# CONTEMPLATIVE TECHNIQUES
# OF HINAYANA

*If the body is not mastered, the spirit is not mastered. If the body is mastered, the spirit is mastered.*

*What a Master does for his disciples, wishing them well by compassion and sympathy, that I have done for you. Here Ananda, there are trees and cells. Practice the meditation, Ananda![1]*

## HINAYANA

Hinayana, or early Buddhism, seeks, by the methods we're about to demonstrate, to make man ascend to Nirvana for his exclusive benefit. The three fundamental principles of this school are:

– The impermanency of phenomena.
– The suffering inherent in phenomena.
– The non-existence of the Self.

There are three fundamental ways to reach Nirvana:

– The observation of ethics.
– The practice of wisdom.
– The practice of concentration.

Hinayana, because of the name itself, which signifies Lesser Vehicle, is often disregarded by Westerners who are ignorant of its meditative practices. In fact, the school of the Lesser Vehicle and of the Greater Vehicle (Mahayana) should not be considered as opposed but rather as complementary. Many masters think that the practice of Hinayana techniques is the most solid foundation on which to base the teaching of Mahayana. These techniques are specially studied to establish mindfulness and to develop perfect mastery of the body and of the mind by leading the human being to a deep consciousness of everything that happens within him. The extremely subtle progression of these techniques leads to detachment, without which no higher state can be reached. Nevertheless, these techniques should not be considered merely as preparations, for they obviously lead to total redemption, as Buddha himself promised his disciples. Simply stated, the beginning graduations are more related to a complete understanding of the contemplative phenomenon as a whole. With this preparation, the more abrupt Mahayanist techniques will not be of any danger. There will be a deep correspondence of level between the depths of being and the actions that release considerable psychic strength. In the East, the three Vehicles, Hinayana, Mahayana and Vajrayana (The Diamond Path), are often considered as three means of reaching the same goal. The first can be compared to a slow but fruitful walk toward knowledge of diverse principles. A fall on the way is normal. The second can be compared to a trip by car; the details of the road blur; an accident can be serious. The third way can be compared to a trip on a supersonic plane. It gives a strong feeling of intoxication in which things are seen from above, the light is violent, and sunrise and the sunset are fantastic; but an accident here is often fatal.

## THE FOUR STAGES OF CONCENTRATION

There are four stages in the practice of concentration, or meditation (samadhi):

1. Concentration that comes from the mastery of the nine Dhyana, which will be shown in detail later. These Dhyana, originating from profound tranquillity, must not be considered as a goal in themselves but as a means of reaching the last deliverance.
2. Concentration that comes from the attainment of extra-sensory perceptions. This means that there is the possibility of perceiving astrological manifestations and phenomena that are not directly apparent to the ordinary man. These perceptions are only a passage, and to remain with them would be dangerous for the development of the other capacities.
3. Concentration that comes from the attainment of mind control. Only the continuous mastery of internal phenomena

and the work of the mind, the profound control of each of its vibrations, of its pulsing creation of images, can lead to the final stages of contemplation. It's not a goal, but a means of penetrating into the profound source.

4. Concentration that comes from the attainment of inner vision or the profound source. It is the last stage, the one that allows crossing the inherent boundaries of perception. The vision that results from it is called the objective vision of reality. It is the last achievement, situated beyond every concept, every opposition.

It is important to understand that the realization of these different stages of concentration cannot always be produced in the order given, and that it is not indispensable to have a perception of astrological phenomena in order to obtain control of the mind or the profound source.

One must also understand that nothing is left to chance in the Oriental systems of meditation. Every stage is realized by the means of special practices, and the objectives are so carefully systematized that one can speak accurately of a true mystical science. It is not a question of wandering in hazy regions where thought cannot penetrate, as we often have the tendency to believe. The contemplative domain is perfectly open, all the roads, all the perils, all the oases are known. Numerous ascetics have travelled them during the ages, and the science of these men is as precise as our mathematics. Everything is predicated, even the abandonment of the last ties, as fragile as they are, which still connect us to the phenomenal world.

For example, it's known that in order to develop the second stage of contemplation, the one of extra-sensory and astrological perceptions, one must concentrate on the contemplation of the nineteenth kasina or the subject of Hinayana meditation: the Light. But before beginning the forty kasina, it is necessary to describe the Four Mindfulnesses that give access to tranquillity, the basis of all meditation.

## THE PRACTICE OF MINDFULNESS

The practice of mindfulness is the key to the total mastery of deliverance. The Buddha emphasized it repeatedly during his talks.

### The Observation of the Body

'There is one thing, monks, which when cultivated and exercised regularly, leads to a profound sense of urgency . . . to the supreme peace . . . to attention and clear understanding . . . to the attainment of the true vision and knowledge . . . to happiness here and now . . . to the attainment of deliverance through wisdom and the fruit of sanctity: it is the mindfulness of the body,' said the Buddha.[2]

*The observation of breathing.* It is necessary, through attention, to be aware of each respiratory movement in order to master it. By this control, one obtains a perfect and peaceful breathing, silent and rhythmical, which is indispensable to the creation of bliss. He who succeeds in mastering breath has already accomplished a very important step. A calm and rhythmical breathing clears the mind and reduces the waves of imagery. The links between mind and respiration are so close that the masters advise changing the respiratory rhythm when a thought begins to unfold and hinders the progress of meditation. There are many respiratory exercises, and it is pointless to list them here. Let's simply say that, in order to obtain balanced breathing, these four phases are enough: inhalation, retention of the breath, exhalation, and emptiness. These follow a balanced rhythm that is slow enough, about four seconds for each step. It is also possible to alternate short and long rhythms. When this exercise is practiced daily, one acquires an automization of the respiratory cycle, and the mind can then concentrate on something else; but this concentration will dissipate if the breath is not regular.

To give you an idea of the peaceful quality that the breath must attain, Tibetan teachers say that a hair placed at the opening of each nostril should not be moved by any of the respiratory movements.

*The observation of the body's positions.* It is necessary to be aware of the least movement of one's body and be able to master and stop it if it doesn't correspond to a higher goal. As in breathing, if one of the body's positions corresponds to a nonelevated mental state, it is advisable to change it in order to break the tie that unites the thought and the position. It is necessary to keep in mind that it is not the 'Self' who is walking, who lies down or sits, but only the aggregate of an illusory existence. It is necessary to grasp behind each attitude the fundamental emptiness inherent in every manifestation.

*The observation of the internal work of the body.* One must be aware of all the movements that are produced inside the body. Through attention, one should arrive at consciousness, and through consciousness, one should arrive at mastery. Concentrate on the heart beat, on the diffusion of blood inside the body, on the contractions of muscles, and on the functioning of the organs. Every time an activity comes to modify the rhythm of the body or makes some organs move, be aware of it. It is also important to realize the illusion of these movements and say to oneself: 'There is a movement here.' And not: 'I am accomplishing a movement here.'

*The observation of the body's impurities.* The body has to be considered a bag of skin containing the following thirty-two substances: hair, body hair, muscles, nails, teeth, skin, sinew, bones, marrow, kidneys, heart, liver, serous membranes, spleen, lungs, intestines, mesenteries, stomach, excrements, brain, bile, digestive juices, pus, blood, oil, fat, tears, sweat, saliva, mucus, sinovial fluids, urine. However, one must neither disregard his body nor give it too much importance, but adopt an intermediary position that consists in watching over its good functioning. As Buddha said, the body is the tool of liberation:

'Truly, I tell you, in this body itself, as moral as it can be and only six feet high, but conscious and endowed with spirit, is found the universe, with its increasings and decreasings and the Road that leads to abandoning it.'

## The Observation of Feelings and Thoughts

By the observation of the feelings that we experience, we ascend the chain of the Twelve Hindrances and realize that suffering is the lot of every feeling, agreeable or not. We must realize their impermanence as their emptiness. In the same way, the person who feels has to be perceived as emptiness. Through observation of the succession and unfolding of thoughts that spring from the mind in a continuous train, it is possible to realize the enormous thinking wave that conditions us; through progressive mastery, it is equally possible to slow this rhythm. It is very difficult to reach the awareness of the continuous movement of the mind, and only a long and regular observation can lead to it. Thoughts jostle, bump, penetrate and engender each other in a whirlwind that has to be reduced to a clear, slender and uniform filament, so that it can be eliminated later by exercises that lead through successive eliminations to the realization of emptiness.

The mind is like a continually jumping-monkey. One can visualize these movements in a passive way without giving them any importance, and by simply keeping in mind the formation and the disappearance of thoughts. Also, one can eradicate a thought as soon as its formation appears consciously. A meticulous analysis allows you to trace the different steps in the production of thought by knowing its origin and source. One should note that thoughts have no existence of their own but are only the fruits of ignorance. It is written in a sutra:

'All phenomena are impermanent, they exist only in our own minds. Therefore, by observing the insubstantial character of everything and by recognizing that all things are nothing else but the objects of the senses, you don't have to dedicate any thought to them.'

### The Observation of Internal Phenomena and the Work of the Mind

We should be aware of the different kinds of feelings that live in us and the way in which they determine action. It's important to establish and to understand how the diverse hindrances produce thought and determine acts. By observing which perception is the cause of an emotion and what is the action of this emotion on our bodies, it then becomes easier to master useless or disastrous reactions. However, it requires much practice before attention becomes constant.

In observing the five Skandhas, contact with which forms the illusions of the Self – namely, physical phenomena, sensation, form, mental activity, and consciousness – we are able to understand which different associations produce illusory phenomena that we can master. Through detailed knowledge of the manner in which these subtle contacts are produced, it becomes possible to intervene even before the hindrances can produce a reaction that could trouble the course of meditation.

In the same way that one can, by this knowledge, abolish the disastrous creations of the mind, one can equally develop fully all beneficial possibilities.

Alexandra David-Neel describes an exercise currently practiced by many Buddhist schools that brings together the practice of the four attentions:

By the end of the day, one recalls the acts he accomplished, the feelings he experienced, and the thoughts he had. This examination is done backwards, which means, it begins at the last feeling that one has experienced, the last action one has accomplished, and the last thought one has had. Then it works gradually up to the first occurrences that followed waking. The most insignificant facts have to be recalled as well as the most important ones. Briefly, the value of recalling our daily mental experiences is simply to teach us not to let anything that our senses have perceived or any idea that has crossed our mind die away without understanding of it.

Buddhism sees memory as a factor of utmost importance. One of its principles is never to forget anything. Everything that has been seen, heard, perceived in any way at all, even only once and for only a minute, has to be registered in memory and never be allowed to disappear.... The examination of a single day is only a beginner's exercise. After a training period whose length varies according to the aptitudes of those who practise it, the examination continues for two days, a week, and then a month, sometimes including not only the incidents registered in wakefulness, but the dreams that appear one after the other during sleep. Certain summaries of the stages of one's past life may include many years and go back to the first days of youth.

... Among the innumerable sensations that affect the organism, only a small amount are consciously revealed and transmitted to the individual's memory; others remain inert, or they are manifested only by impulses and confused inclinations. What we call heredity and atavism can be understood as being attributable to the remote memory of elements that are present in our current person. Thus, some think that through patient training, images that were once invisible can be revealed as on a photographic plate. One can easily agree with the idea of bringing to light a part of our subconscious mind, or even the whole of it, but many will find it difficult to believe in the possibility of recapturing the memory of sensations that have imprinted some of the elements composing our current persons, when they were part of other groups, individuals or things.[3]

If autopsychoanalysis seems absurd to the Westerner, it is because it begins with man, whose understanding is focused on the outside world, and because the attempt is doomed to failure in the framework of the culture and civilization that has shaped us. Therefore, we must resort to an analyst in order to discover our

One day, after having many difficulties with the Darjeeling police who were watching to deport foreigners who remained in this restricted area much longer than they were authorized, Kalo Rinpoche asked me to go and wait for him more than 1,200 miles from there. He would then meet me at Dalhousie, at the foot of the Himalayas, where he had to go to give a series of initiatory rites and meet some anchorite disciples who were coming to get their final teachings. He gave me no approximate date of his coming.

I waited for two months at Dalhousie. In front of my window was a wide expanse of small blue-green valleys and forests that rose slowly to meet the snowy peaks of the Himalayas. The latter blocked the horizon as far as the eye could see and tore the sky with their sharp teeth. One morning, at the bend of a road, I saw, as if in a dream, Kalo Rinpoche on a horse,

surrounded by many monks wearing the orange robe of high ritual. They were moving slowly through a blaze of color. The translucence of the air was giving the colors a brilliance that assaulted the eyes.

Kalo Rinpoche stopped his horse and put his hand on my head, as if we had separated the day before. After an hour's walk, we heard the first sounds of the musical greeting played by the monks from the monastery who were receiving Kalo Rinpoche. Soon, we passed the entrance. On the grass were welcome signs drawn with flour making a path that led to the temple. Scented fires filled the air. The Lamas were waiting with welcoming sashes and cymbals, trumpets, conches, small bells and oboes filled the air with their vibrations.

On the next morning, Kalo Rinpoche began the ceremonies that lasted

until evening, and transmitted to the monks and to the youth who were listening to him, his strength, his science, and his wisdom in the purest tradition of the Kagyupa Masters.

A few weeks later, accompanied by some of his monks, he invited me to follow him, and told me that for the first time I was going to enter the walls of the meditation center. It was there he had to meet the anchorites. A small path led to a tiny building built into the mountain side. From the time of our arrival, we were surrounded by smoke and music.

Kalo Rinpoche was sitting in a room; I saw him lit from behind. We were drinking tea. Filled with delight, some hairy creatures, yogis dressed in white cotton robes, infested with lice, their faces radiant with intense

happiness, came one after the other into the room throughout the day. Some had never come down from their caves – which were isolated in the most inaccessible places of the Himalayas – for more than twenty years. After days of solitary walking, without any forewarning of Kalo Rinpoche's arrival, they had come looking for the ultimate teachings that would allow them to free themselves forever. Some were talking, others were bowing and remained silent. Rinpoche rested his hand on their heads. They stayed still for a long time and then went back to their aloneness, perhaps forever. During the course of this day, I saw faces that I will never forget: the faces of those ascetics who followed the teachings of Milarepa to the letter.

inner workings and decipher them. The Orientals, who have practiced psychoanalysis for centuries, think that the help of an outside person is only beneficial in the case of a close relationship,
such as exists between master and disciple. Even in this case, the
intervention is reduced to a minimum. It relies rather in the practice of techniques and exercises of attention which, little by little,
allow the disciple to descend into himself and to illumine his sub-
conscience. The difference is that, during this slow training, a man
looks into himself while at the same time acquiring the mastery of
his body and mind. This allows him to attain a gradual progressive
enlightenment. He only becomes aware of it when he gains the
necessary strength for his own revelation. It's obviously not the
same for the person analyzed according to Western technique. In
other words, the awareness of the emptiness of phenomena
allows a much more fundamental discovery when perception
scans the depths, and little by little, the states of ecstacy act precisely as a revelation.

The Buddha, after having explained to his disciples the practice
of the Four Mindfulnesses, gives the way of contemplating every
phenomenon coming from these meditations:

1. As impermanent and not as permanent.
2. As painful and not as agreeable.
3. As not-self and not as in oneself.
4. One must go away from it and not take pleasure in it.
5. Consider them without passion and without desire.
6. Cause the end of it and not the origin.
7. Abandon them and don't grasp them.

## THE FORTY KASINA

The kasina, or subjects of meditation, are of two types, and therefore require two different approaches. The first type requires a
deep meditation upon a given subject, accompanied by a profound concentration and a positive realization. The goal of these
kasina is to bring tranquillity to the body and mind by using all the
resources of the intellect. They resolve all phenomena into a profound awareness. The second group demands the same intellectual resources but implies, at a certain moment, the abandonment

of the intellect and sensation, in order to transcend them by a pure vision.

Thus, the Kasina include the whole contemplative scale, from its simplest expression to its supreme level.

1. *The Buddha.* Meditating on the three Buddhas: The historic Buddha as well as the Buddha as spiritual principle, with the firm resolution to become a Buddha by the intensive practice of contemplation. The Buddha Maitreya or future Buddha.

2. *The Dharma.* The teaching of the Buddha has to be meditated upon in order to possess a clear comprehension of it. After the firm understanding by the intellect, it's necessary to realize the teaching by devoting to it one's whole energy.

3. *The Sangha.* The community of monks is not only the guardian of the teachings, but must be their incarnate extension or sensual realization. Only the deliverance of some of its members can avoid the enslavement in dogma and insignificant practices. It is the guide and the living proof of the true teaching.

4. *Morality.* The observation of the five daily rules named by the Buddha: 'Be compassionate and respect all life, even if it be minute. Suppress in yourself malice, greed and anger. Give and receive freely, but don't take anything unduly by means of violence, fraud or dishonesty. Never lie, even on the occasions that seem to you to absolve the lie. Avoid drugs and beverages that trouble the mind. Respect the wife of another man and do not commit any illegitimate or unnatural carnal act.

5. *Generosity.* Do not limit generosity to material gifts, but understand it as a total gift of oneself, bearing in mind the emptiness of the one who gives, the emptiness of the one who receives and the emptiness of what is given. Do not expect anything from the purified act.

6. *Spirits and divinities.* They give access to the interior regions, which are in relationship to their power.

7. *Death.* Death has to be seen as the simple end of an illusory state that we call life and that only is a body in contact with the five skandhas. Death is a sleep without dreams. It is necessary to realize that the Self does not disappear with death, since even during life it is only an illusion. It's necessary to examine how everything subject to birth is equally subject to death, and understand how it continues itself by thirst and attachment through the succession of existences. Nirvana alone is the extinction of thirst.

8. *The body.* The body is considered, as we saw earlier, as a leather bag containing different materials. Here, it's important to consider the position of the body during the practice of contemplation. In general, with slight variation, it is the following: the left foot is placed on the right one. The legs are pulled against the body. The belt is open. A large robe leaves the body free. The left hand is put in the right hand resting on the ankles. The spinal column is neither rigid nor bent. The nose is perpendicular to the navel. The eyes are half closed in order to filter the light. The tongue rests at its natural position.

The correct posture is found by balancing the body gently in order to find equilibrium and perfect stability. Then, the body must be as if fastened to the ground, motionless, massive and unshakeable.

9. *Breathing.* Breathing must be silent. The Great Master Chih-chi of T'ien-t'ai gives the following definition of it: 'In silent breathing, there is no noise, no constraint, and no force is used. There is only a sensation of the tranquillity of our breathing, producing in the mind the impression of security and peace; it's only in practising silent breathing that we can reach samadhi. The other ways of breathing disturb concentration and make it heavy or tire it.'[4]

10. *Tranquillity.* Set to rest all physical and mental activities. The state of well-being that comes from this has to be experienced in the perfection of posture. Nevertheless, it isn't necessary to limit tranquillity to the period reserved for contemplation, but it should be distilled little by little in all other daily activities.

11. *Earth.* The earth is associated with *inertia.* It's one of the four elements of matter. When this contemplation of the element earth in our own body is joined to the three following contemplations, it allows us to feel the impersonal nature of the body. This comparison then brings it closer to inanimate matter.

12. *Water.* Water is associated with *cohesion.* It is the second element that enters into the composition of matter. The contemplation of the liquid elements of the body and of the mixtures of this element with the other three allows one to perceive the insubstantiality of the body.

13. *Fire.* Fire is associated with *radiation.* The principles of contemplation are the same as with those of the other elements.

14. *Air.* Air is associated with *vibration.* The contemplation of this element is practised with the techniques of breathing. The contemplation of the four elements has been recommended by

the Buddha: 'In the same way that a skillful butcher or his appren-
tice kills a cow and cuts it into pieces, and then sits down at the
crossroad of four big roads, so a monk reflects on this same body,
whatever may be its place or its position in relation to these primary elements: in this body there is the element earth, the element
water, the element fire and the element air.'⁵

15. *Analysis of the four elements.* This analysis involves not
only the four elements in the body, but also in the material composition of everything. The passage of this contemplation from
the personal level to the universal puts the emphasis on the unity
of matter that comprises all things.

16. *Blue.* The contemplation of blue is advised for people
whose minds are agitated and tormented, for it has a soothing
effect. It's necessary to practise the contemplation of colors by
examining at first those colors on objects that are found in our vis-
ual field. Then, imagine all the blues of the universe melting
slowly into one abstract and uniform field and, contemplating that
blue, let the awareness slide into a total absorption.

17. *Yellow.* The contemplation of yellow is advised for people
whose minds are obscure, sleepy and indolent. Yellow awakens
the mind and stimulates it. Practise this contemplation like the
preceding.

18. *Red.* The contemplation of red is exciting and more creative
than the contemplation of yellow. The attention is easily fixed on
it, and it provides a sense of well being very favorable to meditation. It's a color very much used in Tantric visualizations for its
striking effect. Practise this contemplation like the preceding
ones.

19. *White.* The contemplation of white is the visible equivalent
of the contemplation of silence. It is the color of peace and the
absence of form. White is an empty color that has all its potentialities in a latent state. This color is equally used in Tantric visualizations. It is the skin color of a great number of divinities.

20. *Light.* The contemplation of light is used mainly by ascetics
who desire to obtain occult powers, which grow quickly when
the attention is perfectly fixed on light. There are all kinds of
techniques. One of the most beneficial seems to be the visualization of a luminous nucleus that traverses the body in a straight
line, from the anus to the top of the skull, while radiating to the different centers of concentration. This visualization can also be performed inside the head by imprinting on the luminous nucleus a

back-and-forth rhythmic movement between a point situated between the eyes and the occiput. The same movement can be performed between the temples, and finally, if the skull is visualized as a sphere, from any point to any other one.

The technique of which we will give the details at the end of this chapter is also based on the contemplation of the luminous nucleus. However, it is done in order to lead to the highest contemplative states. It is possible that during its exercise extra-sensory and astral phenomena of perception appear, but this goal is not pursued. The attainment of emptiness is the ultimate goal.

21. *Sky.* The contemplation of the sky without clouds allows us to reach tranquillity. By looking at the sky for a long time, one distinguishes different layers of blue. By going from one to another, one must let go of the image of the body and allow oneself to fall into space, into emptiness.

22. A human or animal *body*, dead for two or three days, swollen, blue, subject to decomposition. This contemplation, like the nine that will follow, is to point out clearly the nature and the impermanence of the body. It is recommended for fighting against the pleasures of the senses and excessive attachment to the body. It is also recommended for materialistic types so that they comprehend the condition of the physical impermanence of phenomena. Each of these meditations can be accomplished in reality or visualized. (In the East, death is present everywhere, and it is common to see decaying animals, or animals being devoured by vultures. Scenes of cremation are also frequent, and often when the deceased's family cannot buy enough wood to consume the body entirely, half-burnt arms or legs are seen, floating on the sacred river's waters.)

For each of these meditations it is necessary to realize that your own body will undergo the same degradation and that all organisms will equally undergo the same thing. It's also necessary to realize that the dead are only bodies without a Self as are the living.

Moreover, these meditations are recommended for ascetics who want to live alone in desert regions because they provide freedom from fear, from anxiety, from physical suffering, and because they provide great endurance.

23. A *body* slashed by crows, by hawks, by vultures, by dogs, by tigers, by jackals and by worms.

24. A bloody *body* whose skeleton and tendons are visible.

25. A *body* stripped of its flesh, where only bones and tendons remain.

26. A *body* whose remains only include the skeleton and some dried tendons.

27. A *body* whose scattered bones are not in the right order, and the position of which breaks up the image of the body.

28. A *body* reduced to white pieces of bones.

29. A *body* reduced to bones more than a year old.

30. A *body* whose bones are rotten and are no longer identifiable, as a skull, femur, etc. They turn to dust and one can no longer recognize in them the memory of a man's image.

31. *Dust* or earth from which no one can determine the human origin.

32. *Food.* One has to consider it with detachment without falling into the excesses of asceticism. It has to be realized that the thought of food as it is before consumption needs to be contrasted to the decomposition of food during digestion, in order not to attach oneself to taste but only to the nutritive value. The meditator must accept every kind of food with equanimity.

33. *Compassion.* Compassion to all beings of the entire world has to dwell permanently within the meditator. During his meditations, he has to visualize floods of salutary energy that penetrate every creature of the earth under the form of light.

34. *Pity.* The meditator must not isolate himself in a retreat only to devote himself completely to ascetic practices. He has to be constantly aware of the great suffering of humanity and project towards it his waves of light so that he can prevent it from completely moving into darkness. The texts insist strongly on this point: 'Did you tune yourself to the great suffering of humanity, O candidate of the light?'

35. *Sympathetic joy.* One should communicate profound, increasing joy with progress in contemplative practices by spreading it about oneself, like an immense and inexhaustible source that would flood the world.

36. *Composure.* It comes with the realization of tranquillity and of detachment from phenomena that are perceived as being illusory and empty.

37. *The infinity of space.* 'The infinity of space is perceived when one has stopped fragmenting it by distinguishing in himself separate things, and when one has banished from his mind the idea of multiplicity.'[6]

*Family of Tibetan refugees in front of a barbed-wire fence placed by the Indian Government around the residence of the Dalai Lama at Dharamsala, India.*

38. *Infinite awareness.* 'Infinite awareness is perceived when one ceases to confine it to the frame of sensations and perceptions, which are communicated to it by the senses when they contact with external objects.'[7]

39. *The void, non-existence.* 'The void and nonexistence are perceived when one has examined carefully and analyzed all the Dharmas (elements of existence, phenomena) when they have been recognized as being impermanent and destitute of *self*.'[8]

40. *The state where there is neither perception nor absence of perception.* This contradiction is used to express a concept detached from every form of the absolute for this last kasina. It is the total realization.

## THE FOUR MEDITATIONS OF FORM

These four meditations, which relate to form, emerge from the realization of tranquillity. These four stages always indicate a mastery that puts man in contact with the deepest ecstasy.

1. 'A monk detached from objects of the senses and unhealthy ideas enters the *first meditation* born out of detachment and accompanied by the conception of thought both with and without result, and filled with joy and delight. From this joy and delight born from detachment, the body is imbued and so saturated that not a single part of it remains unaffected.'

2. 'After the pacification of both kinds of thought (with and without purpose or result), he acquires the inner tranquillity and harmony of the *second meditation*, which is totally free of thought, born from concentration and filled with joy and delight. From these joys and delights, his body is imbued and so saturated that not a single part of it remains unaffected.'

3. 'After the delight disappears, the monk lives in composure. He is attentive and clearly aware and experiences a happiness in this body, of which the Noble Ones say: "Blessed is he who lives in composure and in attention!" Then he reaches the *third meditation*. From this happiness free of delight, his body is imbued and so saturated that not a single part of it remains unaffected.'

4. 'With the abandonment of pleasure and suffering, and with the previous disappearance of joy and distress, he enters and remains in the *fourth meditation*, which is beyond pleasure and suffering and possesses the purity of attention due to equanimity. He sits down and penetrates this very body with a pure and lucid spirit, so that not a single part of his body remains unaffected. To one who lives in this way, devoted, alert and determined, the memories and the ways of the world vanish. Then his spirit will strengthen internally, will be calm, harmonious and concentrated. In this way, O Monks, you cultivate the attention of the body.'

# Part One

### THE REALIZATIONS OF THE MEDITATIONS OF FORM

*First Meditation*

   —Vigilance, watchfulness
   —Pleasure
   —Silence
   —Quest
   —Enjoyment

*Second Meditation*

   —Purified faith
   —Enjoyment
   —Pleasure
   —Silence

*Third Meditation*

   —Equanimity
   —Wisdom
   —Silence
   —Attention
   —Joy

*Fourth Meditation*

   —Neither suffering, nor pleasure
   —Perfect Attention
   —Equanimity
   —Understanding

### THE FOUR MEDITATIONS WITHOUT FORM

After one has completed the four meditations of form, the four
meditations without form will lead him beyond the world of
phenomena. These four stages of ecstasy correspond with the last
four kasina mentioned above.

   1. The monk no longer has any ideas that relate to phenomenal

existence. He no longer perceives the objects of the senses, such as form, light, sound, odor, and idea. At last, he has no contact with the world of the form. All conception of multiplicity is gone. Thus he remains in the region of infinite space. *This is the first meditation without form.*

2. After the disappearance of endless space, the monk no longer has any contact with space. Then he enters into infinite awareness and remains there. *This is the second meditation without form.*

3. After the disappearance of infinite awareness, the monk sees that all phenomena have no self-existence. He sees that all is nothingness. Thus, he reaches the region of emptiness and remains there. *This is the third meditation without form.*

4. After the disappearance of emptiness, the monk enters the region where there are neither ideas nor the absence of ideas and remains there. *This is the fourth meditation without form.*

To these four steps of ecstasy without form, it is customary to add a last one in order to give another, more precise idea of the limits to be crossed. It is the state of complete rest and of complete cessation, which is the entrance to Nirvana.


## OBSTACLES AND HINDRANCES


In order to fulfill the contemplative conditions mentioned above, man must free himself from the Seven Obstacles and Five Hindrances which are:

—The belief in the existence of Self
—Doubt
—The belief in the effectiveness of rites
—The desire for a future life
—Pride
—Presumption
—Ignorance

—Sensuality
—Anger
—Carelessness
—Mental restlessness
—Scepticism

## INSIGHT INTO THE SOURCE OR THE INNER VISION

The method we are about to relate is little known by Hinayana monks and seems more suited by its characteristics to Mahayana. Nevertheless, it is practised in the Wat Paknam Monastery, in Bangkok, Thailand, and many monks go there to study it. In addition to the monks of the Lesser Vehicle, Zen monks also come to meditate under the direction of the Abbot, which is proof that this method is less than orthodox. Its subtlety and refinement are such that one is easily lost in an intellectual examination of various sorts, which continually occupies the inner state through a long course of insights. This forces the being to go through all the different levels of contemplation, starting from the domain of the form in order to arrive at the final deliverance. A simple explanation of this method covers no less than two volumes: *Samma Samadhi*, Parts 1 and 2, by The Venerable Chao Khun Mongkol–Thepmuni, published in Bangkok in 1962. It isn't possible to give a complete summary of it in a few pages. However, we will describe the first stages.

## THE METHOD INCLUDES THE TEN FOLLOWING INSIGHTS

—Insight into the intangible factors, how they are formed and their true meanings.
—Insight into the endless birth and death of tangible and intangible things from one moment to another.
—Insight into the dissolution of all phenomena.
—Insight into the nature of dangers that need to be avoided.
—Insight into the inherent misery in all the phenomena that take root in desire.
—After the insight into the first five factors, a consequent aversion takes place, which is a preparation for the deliverance.
—Insight into the quest for deliverance by following the Noble Path.
—Insight into the discriminative contemplation that frees by the transcendence of the aggregates of desire.
—Insight into equanimity in which all forms will be perceived in preparing for the final deliverance.
—Insight into the possibility of the transformation of life through which the final deliverance occurs. This is the under-

standing of the Four Noble Truths with all their ramifications and the development of the Middle Road that transcends, at the same time, asceticism and sensuality.


## THE TECHNIQUE IN DETAIL

### 1. The Gross Image of the Body

After having taken the correct position for meditation and having reached tranquillity, concentrate on a point at the middle of the abdomen, two fingers above the navel. Free the mind from every thought and image. Forget breathing. Through concentration, a luminous nucleus will appear. This is assisted by the pronunciation of the mantra *Samma Arahan*, which has to be pronounced slowly and rhythmically. This nucleus is developed in concentration and reaches a diameter of two centimeters. The arrival at this first stage of seeing the luminous sphere can be a lengthy procedure, but it is necessary to persevere until the purity is so complete that it does not hinder further progress. This sphere has to be seen both during the sitting exercise and during the course of daily activities before going further.

—Intensify the concentration on this sphere, which is called the sphere of the first degree. Then it becomes more translucent and luminous.

—Concentrate on it until it becomes completely translucent and still.

—In the center of the sphere appears a nucleus, which through sustained concentration, transforms itself into a sphere called the *Penetrating Attention*.

—Concentrate on it until it becomes translucent and immobile.

—In the center of the sphere a nucleus appears, which through sustained concentration transforms itself into a sphere called *Morality*.

—Concentrate on it until it becomes translucent and immobile.

—In the center of the sphere a nucleus appears, which through sustained concentration transforms itself into a sphere called *Concentration*.

—Concentrate on it until it becomes translucent and immobile.

—In the center of the sphere a nucleus appears, which through sustained concentration transforms itself into a sphere called *Wisdom*.

—Concentrate on it until it becomes translucent and immobile.

—In the center of the sphere a nucleus appears, which through sustained concentration transforms itself into a sphere called *Liberation.*

—Concentrate on it until it becomes translucent and immobile.

—In the center of the sphere a nucleus appears, which through sustained concentration transforms itself into a sphere called *Perception and Knowledge of Liberation.*

—Concentrate on it until it becomes translucent and immobile.

—In the center of the sphere a nucleus appears, which through sustained concentration transforms itself into a refined or astral image of the body of the meditator seen in the lotus position.

## 2. The Refined or Astral Human Form

—Concentrate *on* this form, at the interior of a sphere that can be seen in the center of your abdomen.

—Concentrate on it until it becomes translucent and immobile. In the center of the sphere a nucleus appears, which through sustained concentration transforms itself into a sphere called *Penetrating Attention.*

—Concentrate on it until it becomes translucent and immobile.

—In the center of the sphere a nucleus appears, which through sustained concentration transforms itself into a sphere called *Morality.*

—Concentrate on it until it becomes translucent and immobile.

—In the center of the sphere a nucleus appears, which through sustained concentration transforms itself into a sphere called *Concentration.*

—Concentrate on it until it becomes translucent and immobile.

—In the center of the sphere a nucleus appears, which through sustained concentration transforms itself into a sphere called *Wisdom.*

—Concentrate on it until it becomes translucent and immobile.

—In the center of the sphere a nucleus appears, which through sustained concentration transforms itself into a sphere called *Liberation.*

—Concentrate on it until it becomes translucent and immobile.

—In the center of the sphere a nucleus appears, which through sustained concentration transforms itself into a sphere called *Perception and Knowledge of Liberation.*

—Concentrate on it until it becomes translucent and immobile.

—In the center of the sphere a nucleus appears, which through sustained concentration transforms itself into a gross image of the celestial form sitting in the Lotus position.

The procedure continues in the same manner by going through each Insight by the six spheres: *Penetrating Attention, Morality, Concentration, Wisdom, Liberation*, and *Perception and Knowledge of Liberation*. At the end of each cycle, a new form appears at the interior of the sphere, inside of which the luminous nucleus appears again.

Here are the steps that follow:

3. The gross celestial form.
4. The refined celestial form.
5. The gross form of Brahma.
6. The refined form of Brahma.
7. The gross form of Arupa-Brahma.
8. The refined form of Arupa-Brahma.
9. The gross converted form.
10. The refined converted form.
11. The gross form of the penetrating current.
12. The refined form of the penetrating current.
13. The gross form of the only return.
14. The refined form of the only return.
15. The gross form of the non-return.
16. The refined form of the non-return.
17. The emancipated gross form.
18. The emancipated refined form.

The first eight stages of this meditation lead to the perception of forms that are not visible to the ordinary man. Starting from the astral body, they pass through the diverse forms of the celestial worlds in order to arrive at the Arupa Brahma's world. Arupa means *without form*. Therefore, this world is tied to that realization of a meditative state without form that we spoke about earlier.

The ninth stage marks the passage from the first three stages of concentration (as were described at the beginning of this chapter) to the fourth and last contemplative stage. It signifies the 'converted form.'

The eleventh stage, the penetrating current, reveals the impulse towards the final deliverance. The one who reaches this stage has no more than seven existences to live in Samsara, or the world of illusion.

The thirteenth stage is the one that leaves only one existence to live. The fifteenth stage is the one of non-return to the world of Samsara. He who reaches this stage will be born again into the world of Brahma in order to reach, by a final purification, the seventeenth and eighteenth stages of total emancipation and deliverance. The cycle of rebirth is then finally broken.

The Venerable Chao Khun Mongkol-Thepmuni indicates, however, that the enumeration of penetrations ends because of the lack of space. . .

But it is not the end of the process. Even at that stage, it is still possible to obtain a greater refinement, although the goal has been reached.

*Tibetan Tanka showing the great stages of the Buddha's life.*

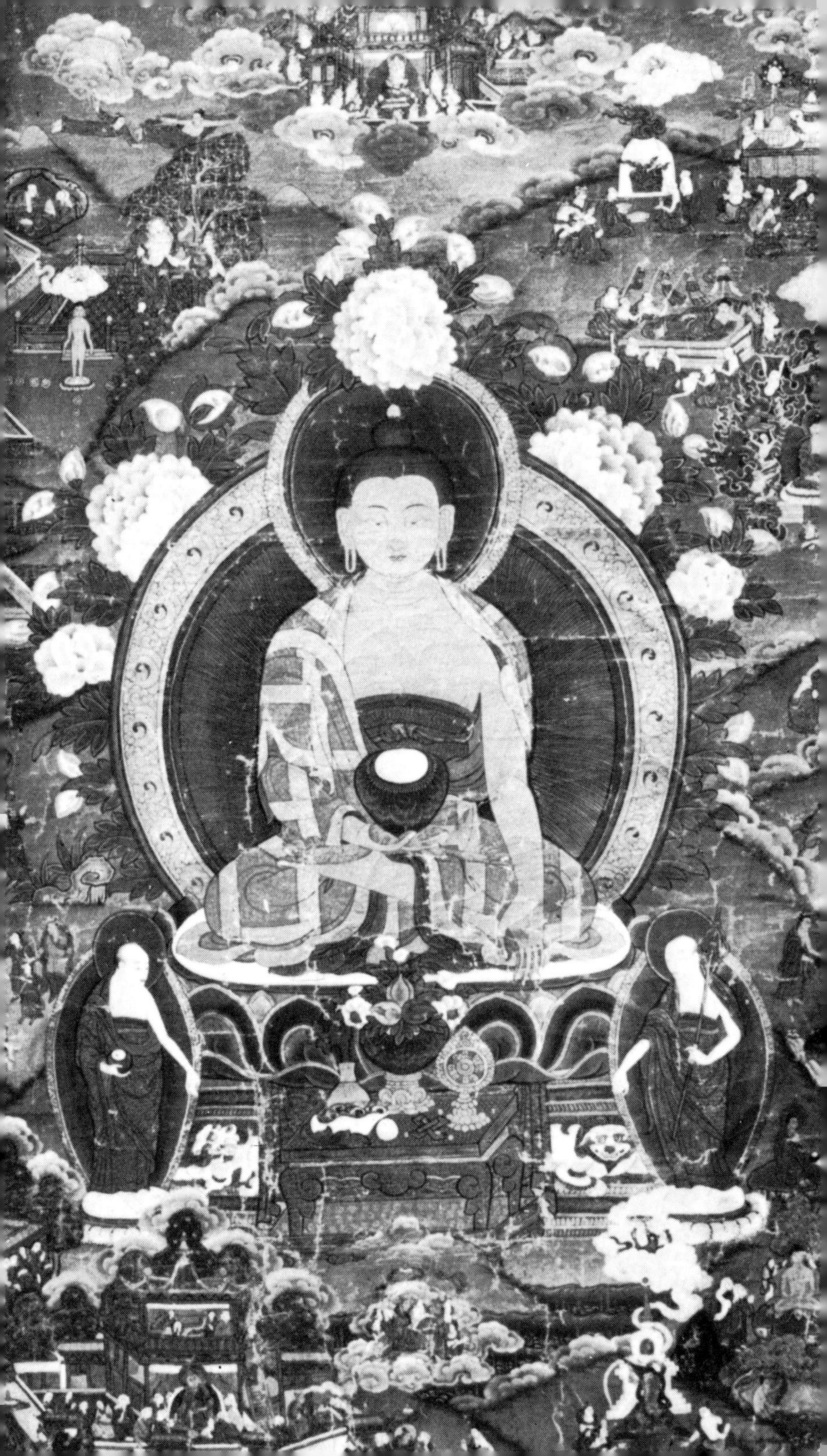

Don't imagine!
Don't think!
Don't analyze!
Don't reflect!
Don't meditate!
Keep your spirit in its natural state.

*Tilopa*

* * *
* *
*

# CONTEMPLATIVE TECHNIQUES
# OF MAHAYANA

## THE LIFE OF MILAREPA

The life of the great Tibetan ascetic Milarepa, who lived in the eleventh century A.D., was written after his death by his beloved disciple, Rechungpa. It consists of different stages of his life, as Milarepa himself told it to his disciples.

It is one of the finest Buddhist texts and also one of the most popular. Through a simple narration fused with great emotional and dramatic intensity, it gives a clear and complete picture of Mahayana, Buddhism of the Greater Vehicle, which leads to the final consequences of the Vajrayana, or Diamond Vehicle.

Two ideas that are the very basis of Mahayana led, little by little, to separate the original school from the new one. First of all, the ideal of Bodhisattva replaces that of Arhat. It preaches the attainment out of the Bodhi, Illumination. This is no longer for the exclusive benefit of the one who is searching for it, but for the benefit of all beings. This universal liberation theme became the goal of each meditator. Then, the theory of emptiness became amplified, little by little becoming the heart itself of the Mahayana doctrine. The schism between the two groups occurred gradually, and it probably existed in the monasteries for a long time. During the second century A.D., the Mahayanist school produced a great number of sutras, and one of the greatest philosophers of all times, Nagarjuna. By the year 150 A.D., he had developed a wide philosophical apparatus that served as foundation for the whole doctrine of the void. Legend tells that the *Prajnaparamita*, or *Great Perfection of Wisdom*, was given to him by the Nagas, mythical snakes that kept the esoteric teaching of Buddha.

This sutra contains the highest teaching of Mahayana. Its original version includes 100,000 verses. Nevertheless, there exists a very condensed version that will be given in this chapter.

About the year 1000, Buddhism disappeared in India, and Mahayana began to flourish in China, in Japan, and in Tibet, becoming more important than the Hinayana. Again it underwent developments that led to Vajrayana and to Ch'an or Zen.

The French translation that we have used to summarize and quote episodes of the life of Milarepa is by Jacques Bacot.[1]

## BIRTH

In August 1052, White-Garment gave birth to a son, while her husband, Trophy-of-Wisdom, a rich merchant, was in the north of Tibet selling products bought in the south. The son's name was Good-News. Four years later a daughter was born and named the Happy Patronness. The family lived in the village of Kyagnatsa in a splendid fortified house called Four Columns and Eight Beams.

## YOUTH

Good-News had just turned seven. His father was stricken with a terrible disease. After putting his family and his assets under the protectorship of the uncle and aunt of his son, he died. He was loved by all the inhabitants of the village. When the uncle and aunt took possession of the fortune of Trophy-of-Wisdom, they reduced his wife, his son and his daughter to misery and slavery. The people of the village mourned the fate of this family stricken by the most cruel poverty. The family consoled itself by repeating the Tibetan proverb: 'While the false master is the master, the true master is at the door like a watch dog.'

When Good-News reached maturity, his uncle and aunt refused to restore his wealth. The uncle mockingly said: 'If you are rich, declare war on us. If you are poor, cast spells over us.'

## MISDEEDS

Good-News was sent by his mother to the village of Mithongeka, where a magician taught him how to read. Then, she asked her son

*Milarepa. Engraved wood coming from the monastery of Tengpoche,
located on the road to Everest (Nepal)*

to depart and to learn the magic art of casting spells and making
hail in order to destroy their enemies. She sold half of her field,
and bought presents for the Lama. One present was a turquoise
jewel called Great-Twinkling-Star and the other a white horse called Lion-Who-Has-No-Bridle. Her son found travelling companions and before his departure she told him: 'If you come back
without manifesting in the country some signs of your magic, I,
your old mother, will kill myself before your eyes.'

After a long trip, Good-News and his companions came before a
well-known Lama called Man-of-Nyag-Irritated-Vanquisher-Who-

Teaches-Evil. After offering gold obtained from the sale of the
horse and turquoise gem, Good-News said to the Lama: 'I also offer
you my body, my word and my heart.' For the first time, the Lama
saw a disciple who was offering himself totally to him. After a test,
the Lama initiated him. He gave him two formulas: one to make
someone die, and the other to make him lose consciousness. Then
he advised him to go and see another Lama called Ocean-of-Vir-
tue-from-Kulung, who in exchange for his formulas, would give
him the one that could make hail fall. After they had built an isolated cell together, the Lama initiated him.

The spell was cast. Fourteen days later, the gods set on the mandala the heads of thirty-five victims and their bloody hearts. The
uncle and aunt were spared. The whole family of the uncle and
aunt were killed at a feast during which their house fell to pieces.

Good-News came back home and released the hail, which
destroyed the harvest of those who had planned to stone him and
his family.


## THE CONVERSION


One day, the Lama was grieving because he had practiced witch-
craft and the casting of spells all his life. He asked Good-News to
devote himself from now on to the search for the pure doctrine,
and entrusted him with presents, a yak and a piece of fine cloth,
telling him to go to Lama Rontunlaga in order to receive his teaching.

After the Lama had communicated his doctrine to him, he saw
that his disciple was not practicing assiduously. He knew that
Good-News had to go to the one who would be his true Master,
the terrible Marpa, disciple of the great Indian pandit Naropa, with
whom he had been in communication during several lives. 'As
soon as I heard the name of the interpreter Marpa, I was filled with
an inexpressible happiness. In my joy, my hair stood on end. I sob-
bed in deep worship. Closing my soul on a single thought, I took
my provisions and a book. Without allowing my thought to be dis-
tracted by any other thing, I began my journey, endlessly repeating: When will it be? When will I see the Lama face to face?' The
night before his disciple arrived, Marpa saw his Master Naropa in a
dream; when he awakened, he noticed that his wife had had the

same premonitory dream. He then left his hermitage and went to work in a field.

Good-News arrived and saw him: 'On the edge of the road, there was a tall and stout monk, with big eyes and a terrible look, plowing a field. As soon as I saw him, I was filled with an indescribable joy and an inconceivable happiness. What I saw took hold of me and I stopped dead in my tracks.

After the field was ploughed, Good-News found himself face to face with the monk who was none other than the terrible Marpa. 'Then I prostrated myself and put his foot on my head: Precious Lama, I am a great sinner of Gnimalatod. I offer you my body, my word and my heart. I am asking you for food, clothes and your teaching. Can you teach me the way that leads from this life to perfection? The lama replied: 'If you are a great sinner, don't come and tell me about it. By sinning, you did not offend me.'

## THE TESTS

Marpa asked Good-News to send hail over the two regions his disciples had to cross, where they were experiencing many attacks.

Later, he told him that the doctrine of the Great Naropa allows one to reach Bodhi from this life, but that it is not in exchange for some hailstones. Marpa then asked that the mountaineers who attacked his disciples be punished. Good-News saw to it. The mountaineers killed each other in a brawl. From that day on, Marpa called his disciple Great Magician. Good-News asked for the formula of Marpa's master, Naropa. Marpa told him that such a formula can only be given to those who are purified.

The tests began. Great Magician, in order to receive the doctrine, had to build a round tower. When the construction was half completed, Marpa asked him to take each stone back to its place.

After that, Great Magician built a half-moon tower. Marpa made him destroy it.

A triangular tower was then built and destroyed. Great Magician suffered. His body was but a wound. The Lama's wife comforted him with her love and her pity. Marpa had never treated a disciple so harshly. After a few days of rest, Marpa gave Great Magician his first teachings. Those were the ones that everyone received but were not the esoteric doctrine. Later, he took him to the mountain and told him to build a nine-storey-tower with a pinnacle. Then he would give him the initiation. While the second floor was being finished, Marpa asked him to remove one foundation stone placed without his knowledge. When the enormous stone that had been rolled by three men was removed, Marpa asked that it be put back in the building.

Great Magician then came to receive the initiation with another disciple. The Lama asked him where his gifts for receiving the secret doctrine were and then chased him away by beating him.

The next morning, Marpa asked his disciple to build a low gallery with a sanctuary; after that he would give him the initiation.

Great Magician came again in order to receive the teaching with another disciple. This time the Lama's wife had given him presents for the Master. Marpa refused the gifts that already belonged to him and kicked his disciple out. The next morning, he told him to finish the gallery and to add a tower to the building. The Great Magician's back became nothing more than an infected wound. The Lama's wife pleaded in his favor. Then Marpa received his disciple and said to him:

'The twelve tests of my Master Naropa were such that even the small ones surpassed yours. And he imposed on his body twenty-four mortifications other than these. As for myself, without thinking of liking my life or of managing my wealth, I handed them over to my Master, Naropa. That's why, if you desire the doctrine, be modest and go on with the work of the tower.'

While he was working, the Lama came to watch and shed tears over such a submission.

With the help of the Lama's wife, Great Magician feigned a departure. Marpa wasn't tricked. He beat him unmercifully. His protectress then gave him a present of a turquoise gem that she had been secretly keeping, but Marpa kept the stone and thanked his wife instead of Great Magician.

Great Magician ran away, and this time without telling anybody. Marpa wept over the disappearance of his beloved son and implored the gods to bring him back. His prayers were heard.

After his disciple's return, Marpa asked for a final construction. Discouraged, Great Magician ran away again. The Lama's wife gave him gifts for one of Marpa's disciples who had become an instructor. This disciple, Gnogpa, gave him an intiation, but all progress was impossible for Great Magician without leave from his guru. He went back to Marpa, who treated him so cruelly that he dreamt of suicide.

Finally, one day Marpa sent for him and explained the meaning of the tests that he underwent as well as his attitude, which despite appearances had always been that of a Bodhisattva.

That same evening, Great Magician received the ordination as well as the name of Mila-Trophy-of-Wisdom.

Marpa drew the mandala of the seventy-two spirits and gave his beloved son the profound initiation.


### THE MEDITATION


Mila then remained eleven months walled in a cave with a lamp on his head, and practised meditation day and night. Then Marpa came to get him. They went down to the Hermitage. The mother cooked a banquet for the father and the son. Mila then revealed what he understood from the teaching:

'I understood that the Greater Vehicle was to sacrifice oneself through the virtues of pity and compassion for the cause of all creatures.'

After having spoken of the teaching in the way he understood it, Mila returned to his cave and meditated assiduously. Marpa, in spite of his old age, again went to India to receive a principle that he did not know. Naropa was dead, but he would appear to his disciple and give him the final teachings. When Marpa came back, he asked his disciples to describe their dreams in order to determine who would transmit the Kagyupa doctrine to modern times. Mila was chosen by the gods. Marpa conferred all the initiations on his disciples and divided the doctrine among them. Each one would have to insure the survival of what he received.

The great disciples then departed and spread the doctrine. Only Mila remained a few more years with Marpa. Soon, it was time for the separation. The mother prepared a banquet. She was shaken by grief. Marpa realized that they would never see each other again.

'Having said this, she increased her mourning twofold. As for me, my tears were unbearable. The Lama himself wept. Master and disciple, we suffer in our mutual affection and our mourning leaves us speechless.'

Mila returned to his village. The house was in ruins. His mother was dead. His sister had left to lead a wandering beggar's life. He felt great pain.

A monk during
his meditation
executes a series
of mudra, sym-
bolic gestures of
the hands com-
municated by the
Guru, which put
the meditator in
direct rapport
with the object of
his contempla-
tion.

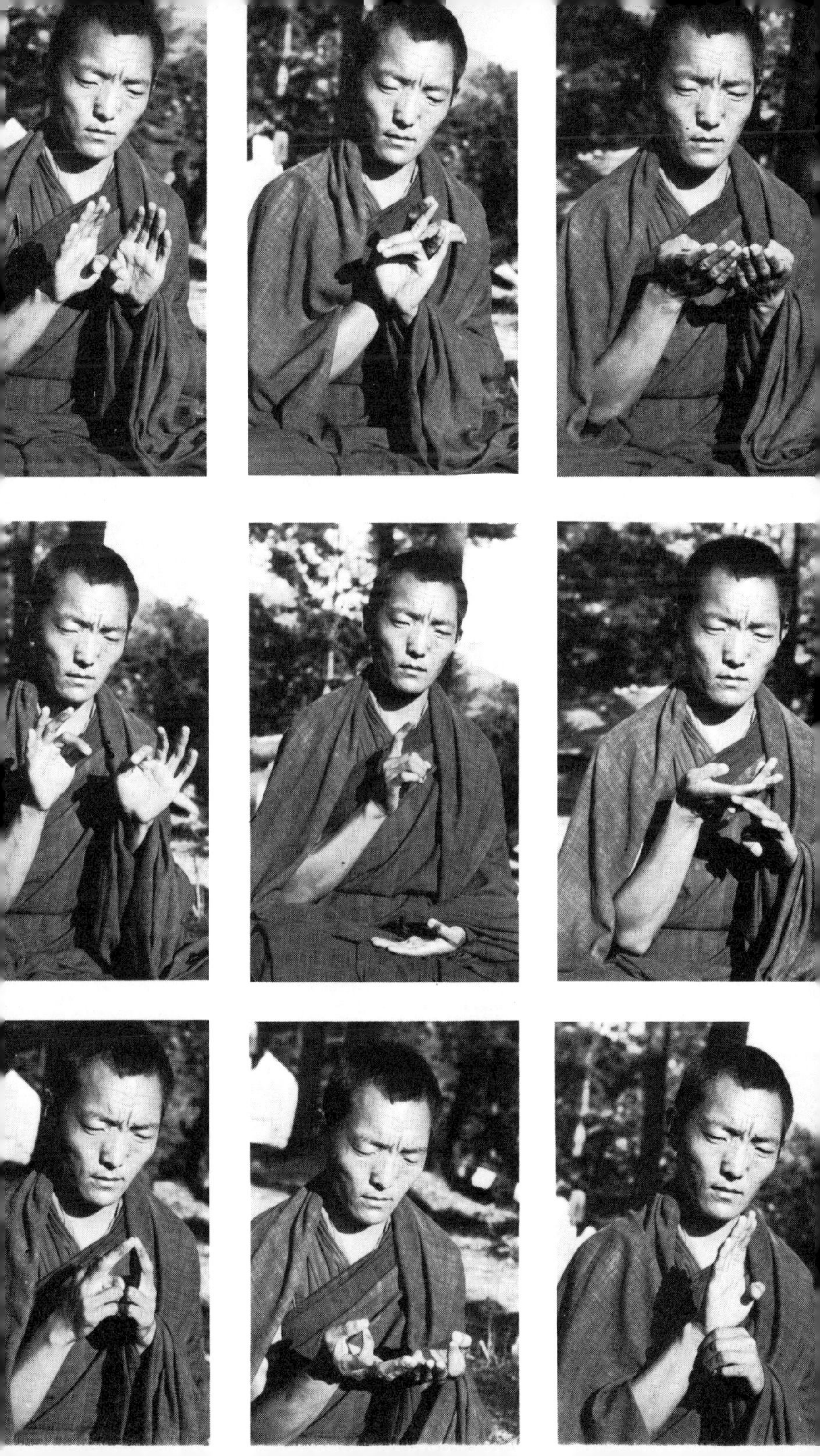

He went to a cave and spent many years living on nettles. His body grew weak and turned green. Then one day some peasants fed him meat and vegetables. He began to feel his strength returning.

After some time, his sister Peta found him, weak and sick. She fed him and Mila regained his strength:

'During the day, I was changing my body at will. My mind was imagining innumerable transformations, flying in the sky with the two parts of my body unmatched. During the night, in my dream, I could freely and without obstacle explore the entire universe from hell to the highest point. And transporting myself under hundreds of different corporeal and spiritual forms, I visited each one of the Buddha's different heavens, and listened to their teachings. I could teach the Law to a host of creatures. My body was covered with flames and spewing water at the same time.'

Milarepa began to teach by singing poems.


## THE HERMITAGES


Then Milarepa retired into caves, many of which are found in Nepal, and within which his successors are still meditating today. In all of these places, he received disciples. He taught and gave the various initiations to advanced Lamas.

During these long retreats, he performed a great number of miracles. Some reached supreme knowledge only by listening to his songs.

To Geshe Tsaphoua, who came with the intention to defeat him during a debate, he offered this song:

Greetings to the interpreter Marpa.
May he bless me so that I can avoid this controversy.
May the benediction of my Lord penetrate my spirit.
May my spirit not be troubled by these things.
Having meditated on gentleness and on compassion,
I have forgotten the difference between myself and others.
Having meditated on my Lama in the highest part of my skull,
I have forgotten those who command by authority.
Having meditated on my Yidam at the same time,
I have forgotten the coarse world of the senses.
Having meditated on the principles of the oral tradition,
I have forgotten books and logic.

Having kept the science of the universal,
I have forgotten the illusions of ignorance.
Having meditated on the formation of the Three Bodies in oneself,
I have forgotten hope and fear.
Having meditated on this life and the life after,
I have forgotten the fear of birth and death.
Having tasted the joys of solitude,
I have forgotten the opinion of my brothers and friends.
Having composed verses for posterity,
I have forgotten to take part in the controversies of doctrine.
Having meditated on what has neither beginning nor negation nor place,
I have neglected all the forms of convention.
Having considered the Nirvanic body of appearances,
I neglected to meditate on the creations of the mind.
Having truly disclaimed discourse,
I have forgotten the use of hypocrisy.
Having chosen the body and the speech of the humble,
I have forgotten the pride and arrogance of important personalities.
Having made of my body my own monastery,
I have forgotten the monastery of the city.
Having adopted the spirit without the letter,
I have forgotten to analyze the words.

The Geshe then tried to have Milarepa poisoned. At eighty-four years of age the Sage would drink the poison that was destined for him: he would know that his time was over, and that if he was to die, it would not be because of the poison of men. In order to convert the Geshe, he transfered his sickness to a door, which warped and decayed. The Geshe still did not have faith, so he gave him a portion of the illness and removed it from him as soon as he was penetrated by the Light.

After having sung, he encouraged his disciples to become absorbed in contemplation. Then, remaining motionless, he left his human shell.

## NIRVANA

A series of miracles then shook the universe, and on his funeral pyre, Milarepa appeared in his celestial form and offered a departing chant to his assembled disciples:

In the ocean of the transmigration of the three worlds,
The unreal body is the great sinner.

One is so conscious about food and clothing that
There is no self-denial in the world.
Renounce the world, O Rechungpa.

In the city of unreal bodies the unreal soul is the great sinner.
Submitted to the flesh and to the blood of the body,
It never has insight into its own nature.
Distinguish the nature of the soul, O Rechungpa.

At the borders of mind and matter,
The knowledge created by oneself is the great shame.
Passing suddenly from one impression to the other,
It has no time to realize
That these impressions do not have their own origin.
Stand still on the firm ground of the non-objectivity of things.

In the mutual dependence of this life and the other,
Memory in hell is the great criminal.
Deprived of body, it searches for the association of a body.
It has no time to discover the unreality of the sensory world.
Finish in void, O Rechungpa.

In the deceiving city of the six classes of beings,
The blindness of sin is immense.
The spirit follows the impulse of love and hatred.
It has no time to perceive the equal inanity of things.
Reject love and hatred, O Rechungpa.

In the midst of immaterial space,
The accomplished Buddha creates deceitful images,
He has taught through the seduction of the visible world.
The mind has no time to conceive the real world.
Neglect this indirect teaching, O Rechungpa.

Play together, like a unique trinity,
Lamas, Yidam and gods,
All reunited in single unity.
Contemplation, meditation and consumption.
Accustom yourself to do only one thing.
In this life, in the next and in limbo.
This is my last teaching.

This is the end of my testament:
After, there is nothing more, O Rechungpa.

## THE IDEAL OF BODHISATTVA
## AND THE EMPTINESS OF PHENOMENA

Although the elements of Mahayana and of Vajrayana are blended in the life of Milarepa, he demonstrates the best and simplest introduction to the Buddhism of the Greater Vehicle. As this story indicated, the school of Mahayana rests upon two principles. First of all, there is the ideal of the Bodhisattva, which widens the original ideas by offering as an example the one who wishes to enlighten all of humanity along with himself in the realization of Nirvana. Through love, the Bodhisattva takes upon himself the human condition that he intends to free from suffering. This idea is not really a creation of Mahayana. In fact, it always existed. But Mahayanists give it an absolute priority over all quests that are exclusively personal. A text of the *Prajnaparamita* defines this ideal:

The Bodhisattva are doers of what is difficult. They are the great beings who undertake the task of gaining Supreme Illumination. They do not want to attain their own private Nirvana. On the contrary, they travelled through the highly painful world of existence, and yet remained desirous of gaining Supreme Illumination. They do not tremble in front of birth and death. They started their journey for the benefit of the world, for the happiness of the world, and through compassion for the world. They have taken this decision: We want to become a shelter for the world, a refuge for the world, a place of rest for the world, the final comfort of the world, the islands of the world, the lights of the world, the guides of the world, the means of salvation of the world.[2]

The second principle of Mahayana is the conception of the fundamental emptiness of all phenomena as well as the emptiness of the Self. In the practical realization and in the elaboration of contemplative techniques that we are now going to discuss, everything is centered on the double realization of the Bodhisattva ideal and of the profound emptiness inherent in all manifestation.

In order to reach this double goal, Mahayana particularly emphasizes the importance of the master, who allows the disciple to follow a very difficult path yet gives him all the chances of success. The master does not yet possess the absolute primacy that the Vajrayana gives him, but he is the indispensable link in the chain that slowly develops and leads to the final liberation. The master is the intermediary to whom the disciple offers his body, his word, and his spirit as Milarepa did.

In order to describe the life of a disciple who devotes himself to realization, we have selected some of the precepts of the *Supreme Path of the Disciples*, a very popular collection that most of the Tibetan monks know by heart:

—Having obtained a free and gifted human body, which is a blessing, it would be a waste to foolishly exhaust this life.

—Since the holy Guru is the guide on the Path, it would be a waste to be separated from him before attaining Illumination.

—Since the flower of youth is the period of the development of the body, word and mind, it would be a waste to spend it in vulgar indifference.

—Having understood one's own capacities, it is necessary to have a definite plan of action.

—The mind imbued with love and compassion in thought and action must always be directed to the service of every living being.

—Study impartially the teachings of great sages of all sects.

—Constantly be attentive, whether walking, sitting, eating or sleeping.

—What comes by itself, without being asked for, is a divine gift, which should not be avoided.

—One should know that all visible phenomena are illusory, thus unreal.

—Having chosen a religious instructor, divorce yourself from selfishness and follow scrupulously his teachings.

—Having obtained the practical knowledge of spiritual things and accomplished the great Renunciation, do not allow your body, your word or your mind to became disorderly, but observe the three vows of poverty, of chastity and of obedience.

—One must persevere in solitude until the mind has obtained the yogic discipline.

—Meditation without sufficient preparation in listening to and studying the Doctrine can lead to the error of losing oneself in the shadows of unawareness.

—The cessation of the movement of thought can be mistaken for the tranquillity of the infinite mind, which is the true goal.

—To be clever in precepts but to ignore the spiritual experiences that come from their application, is like being a rich man who has lost the key to his treasure, which is bankruptcy.

—A method of meditation giving the power to concentrate the mind on anything is indispensable.

—To differ from the multitude in all thought and all action is the sign of the superior man.

—Considering that visible or existing phenomena are always transitory, changeable, unstable, and particularly, that the life of the world cannot provide either reality or permanent gain, it is useless to dedicate oneself to worldly activities without true benefit rather than to the search for Divine Wisdom.

—A charitable act is done for oneself. One is content with simple things and frees oneself from the thirst for worldly possessions.

—For a superior intelligence, the best meditation is to remain in mental stillness. Here the mind is empty of thought, knowing that the thinker, the object of thought and the act of meditation constitute an inseparable unity.

—For a religious devotee to try to reform others instead of reforming himself is a grave error.

—One should have the capacity for fixing his mind on a single thought, just as a mother who has lost her only son will do.

—One has to unmask the illusion of dualism just as one would uncover the deceptions of a liar.

—If the emptiness of mind has been realized, it is no longer necessary to listen to or to meditate on religious teachings.

—For him who has reached the unadulterated state of Purity, it is not necessary to meditate on the Path or the methods to travel it, for he has reached the goal.

—If all phenomena are recognized as illusory, it is not necessary to seek or to reject anything.

—A momentary insight into Divine Wisdom, originating from meditation, is more precious than any amount of knowledge obtained from simply listening to or thinking about religious teachings.

—For him who has realized Reality, it is the same thing to dwell on an isolated mountain or to come and go.

—For him who has abandoned the life of the world and devoted himself to the practice of spiritual truths, it is the same thing either to follow or not follow conventional codes of conduct.

—As there is neither a method of following nor an entity who is following the Path, the expression *Path* is purely figurative.

—It is a great joy to realize that the spirit of all living beings is inseparable from the Universal Spirit.

—It is a great joy to realize that the Path of Liberation, which all the Buddhas have followed, is always there, always similar and always open to those who are ready to enter it.[3]


## CONCENTRATION ON ONE UNIQUE OBJECT


In silence and aloneness, the disciple of the School of Mahayana strives to reach the tranquillity of body, word and mind in realizing the six rules of Tilopa:

—Don't imagine.
—Don't think.
—Don't analyze.
—Don't reflect.
—Don't meditate.
—Keep your spirit in its natural state.

The concentration on only one object is the method that allows this realization. This unique concentration is, in general, divided into two types of exercises: Those that use rhythmical breathing and those that don't.

## 1. Concentration with free breathing

For this first stage of concentration, the masters recommend, in general, the use of a simple object; a small stone, the flame of a candle, the reddish end of a burning incense stick or any small object will do on the condition that it can easily be distinguished from the environment.

After having directed a prayer to his master and implored his waves of graciousness, the disciple concentrates his mind on the object and centers his thought in order to prevent it from wandering. He does not identify with the object but, in the correct posture, he looks at it and sets aside all physical and mental activity. When the mind is agitated by waves of thoughts, one should practice in an enclosed place, a hermitage or cell. If, on the contrary, the mind is lazy, it is then necessary to meditate in open air, in an elevated place from which one can see endlessly, so as to stimulate the energy.

After having successfully experienced this first method of centering, the disciple approaches the triple contemplation of the body, word and mind of the Buddha symbolized by his image, the mantra, and a luminous point. We will come back in detail to this technique and its developments in the next chapter, which is devoted to Vajrayana.

## 2. Concentration with rhythmic breathing

These techniques have a capital importance, for they open the door to the perfect mastery of breathing, which alone allows the ascetic to reach the highest ecstasy. The mastery of breath is developed in a parallel way to the mastery of thought, because there exists a deep bond between these two functions. Anyone can become aware of this bond; all it takes is changing the respiratory rhythm in order to change the mental condition. In the process of meditation, this is one of the techniques used for eliminating the formation of thoughts and memories that prevent concentration.

After having corrected his posture, the meditator concentrates on the inhalation and exhalation of breath, while establishing a rhythmic movement. The movement can be accomplished in two steps:

Inhalation–Exhalation.

Or in four steps:

Inhalation–Retention–Exhalation–Emptiness.

The simplest method is to count rhythmically, allowing oneself to be absorbed in the rhythm. It is equally important to follow the air during its trip inside the body. Every movement has to be slow and imperceptible.

By practicing these techniques, the disciple develops awareness, and at the same time masters mind and body. He is preparing for the practice of concentration such as it was defined by Tilopa.

## CONCENTRATION WITHOUT OBJECT

While the preceding methods relied on an object in order to attain emptiness, the three methods that follow allow mastery of the flux of automatic thought, and detachment in order to know ecstasy.

## CUTTING THE ROOT OF THOUGHT

It is extremely important to be aware of the rhythm of thought as it moves within us, creating an indefinite number of impetuses and preventing us from realizing the fundamental emptiness of our mind.

Once this is clear, one must from the beginning of meditation cut off all thought as soon as it arises. This is called the method of cutting the root.

## NOT REACTING TO THOUGHTS

This method does not attempt to suppress the object of thought, but simply brings an indifference and neutrality to the unfolding of the thought process. The meditator does not dwell on the thoughts that are produced in him but lets them unfold indifferently, as if it were a question of something strange happening within him. Without making any effort to stop thoughts, the meditator separates them from the continuous flux and pays no attention to them.

## REACHING THE NATURAL STATE OF THE SPIRIT

This last method is one of perfect equilibrium that allows the spirit to recover its unstained state. The meditator must neither stretch nor relax his mind. In this state that avoids any extreme that causes fatigue, tension or relaxation, the meditator keeps his spirit detached from ideas, in perfect contemplation. His attitude toward visions that are then produced is the same; he does not fix himself in them, he does not try to push them aside, and he simply remains in the state of ecstasy, without in any manner attaching himself to the phenomena that are produced.

## THE SIX EXERCISES OF NAROPA

The six exercises of Naropa are interesting because they offer a conception of yoga that is highly streamlined. Only the exercises that really open the body and mind to the contemplative practice are retained.

1. Sitting in the lotus position, place the closed fists on the knees and rock the shoulders from right to left. The nervous knot of the navel will be undone by this exercise.
2. While remaining in the lotus position, make the head describe circles as large as possible. Bend the head from

front to back. The nervous knots in the head and throat will be undone by the practice of this exercise.

3. While remaining in the lotus position, open the hands and place them on the knees, and swing the chest concentrically. The nervous knots in the chest will be undone by this exercise.

4. Stretch the arms and then vigorously shake them. Then, sitting down, raise the legs in front of you and shake them also. The nervous knots in the four limbs will then be dispersed.

5. Leap into the air, cross the legs in the lotus position and fall back into position, ready for meditation. Then raise yourself up by a series of leaps. Each leap has to be accomplished by a rapid twist of the chest. The nervous knots in the whole body will then be undone.

6. Massage the whole body in order to calm the nerves and to put them back in place.

## THE MEDITATIONS ON EMPTINESS

If the techniques that follow require discrimination, it is because they lead the meditator, by the game of denials, to non-thought and to emptiness. Of course, it is not enough only to intellectually examine the following statements in order to realize the profound emptiness of all phenomena. It is a question of attaining a complete fusion of the entire being through the given systems.

## THE MEDITATION ON THE FOUR PHASES
## OF THE MAHAPARANIRVANA SUTRA

—Not born from self
—Not born from other
—Not born from both self and other
—Not born from a cause

## THE MEDITATION ON THE EIGHT OPPOSED NEGATIVES

—Non-production
—Non-extinction

—Non-annihilation
—Impermanence
—Non-unity
—Non-diversity
—Non-coming
—Non-departure

### THE MEDITATION ON THE FOUR VOIDS

—Emptiness of the personal self
—Emptiness of other selves
—Emptiness of the Dharma
—Emptiness of form and phenomena

### EMPTINESS ACCORDING TO THE DIAMOND SUTRA

What we call reality must be considered as having no more reality
than:

—A dream
—An illusion
—A bubble
—A cloud
—A shadow
—An hallucination

## THE MEDITATION ON CAUSALITY

This meditation is the deep realization of the Twelve Hindrances as they were explained in Chapter 2.

## THE MEDITATION ON THE GREAT COMPASSION
## COMING FROM EMPTINESS

We are one with all humanity. Emptiness is in us as it is in each of them. Only great compassion, born from emptiness, can bring perfect love and save all beings. This is the responsibility of the Bodhisattva.

## THE MEDITATION ON THREEFOLD EMPTINESS

We have to realize that in each of our actions there is a threefold emptiness: the one who acts, his mode of action and the goal of his action.

## THE MEDITATION ON RESPIRATION

When the meditator exhales, he distributes his light to the whole world in order to save all beings. When the meditator inhales, he takes upon himself all the suffering and evil of the world and uses this force to destroy the illusion of the existence of Self.

## THE NON-MEDITATION ON RESPIRATION

The meditator breathes out into emptiness.
   The meditator breathes in into emptiness.

## THE SEVENTEEN KINDS OF EMPTINESS

   —Interior Emptiness
   —Exterior Emptiness
   —Interior and Exterior Emptiness
   —Empty Emptiness
   —Great Emptiness
   —Composed Emptiness
   —Noncomposed Emptiness
   —Absolute Emptiness
   —Infinite Emptiness
   —Emptiness without Beginning or end
   —Emptiness that contains everything
   —Emptiness empty by itself
   —Universal Emptiness
   —Emptiness that escapes thought

—Emptiness without characteristics
—Emptiness without properties
—Emptiness of matter

Finally, in order to give an idea of this notion of emptiness, which is so difficult to grasp, here is one of the ultimate teachings of Mahayana, which is a condensed version of the *Prajnaparamita*, which includes one hundred thousand verses in its original version.

## DISCOURSE ON THE ESSENCE OF THE PRAJNAPARAMITA[4]

The Victorious One was on the Mountain of the Assembly of Vultures and a great number of the devout and Bodhisattvas surrounded him.

Buddha had just left his profound meditation; he greeted the noble Chenrezig (Avalokiteshvara) and then asked this question:

How must a son or daughter of a noble family behave in accordance with the *Prajnaparamita?*

Chenrezig answered him:

The Bodhisattva must see it as follows:

The five constituent groups (skandhas) are by themselves empty.

Form is emptiness. Emptiness is form.

Form is nothing else but emptiness.

Emptiness is nothing else but form.

Sensation is emptiness. Emptiness is sensation. Sensation is nothing else but emptiness. Emptiness is nothing else but sensation.

It is the same with perceptions, mental preparations, and consciousness-knowledge. Each of them is emptiness, and emptiness is in them. They are nothing else but emptiness, and emptiness is nothing else but what they are.

Sariputra, all things being empty, there are no characteristics, no birth, no obstruction to birth. There is no impurity. There is no rejection of impurity; there is nothing completely.

Sariputra, if this is so, then in the emptiness there is neither form, nor sensation, nor perception, nor mental formations, nor consciousness-knowledge. There is neither eye, nor ear, nor nose, nor tongue, nor body, nor mind.

There is neither sound, nor odor, nor flavor, touch, nor things.

There is neither the domain of the eye, nor the domain of the other senses, nor that of the mind.

There is no ignorance, no destruction of ignorance, no aging or death, no obstruction to old age and death.

There is neither pain, nor its origin, nor its suppression.

There is neither the Way, nor the obtainment of something nor the non-obtainment.

Sariputra, the Bodhisattvas behave according to the teachings of the *Prajnaparamita*, which point to the way of the non-obtainment. Consequently, they are free from darkness and fear, having gone beyond false views.

Likewise, the Buddhas, according to the teachings of the Bodhisattva, in the three periods, have attained perfect accomplishment, which has nothing above it, and they have thus become Buddhas.

And here is the secret principle, without equal, the principle that calms all suffering, the truthful principle, the *Prajnaparamita*'s principle:

Gaté, gaté, paramgaté
parasamgaté, Bodhi, swaha!

Homage to you, Knowledge that has gone,
Gone beyond and beyond the beyond.

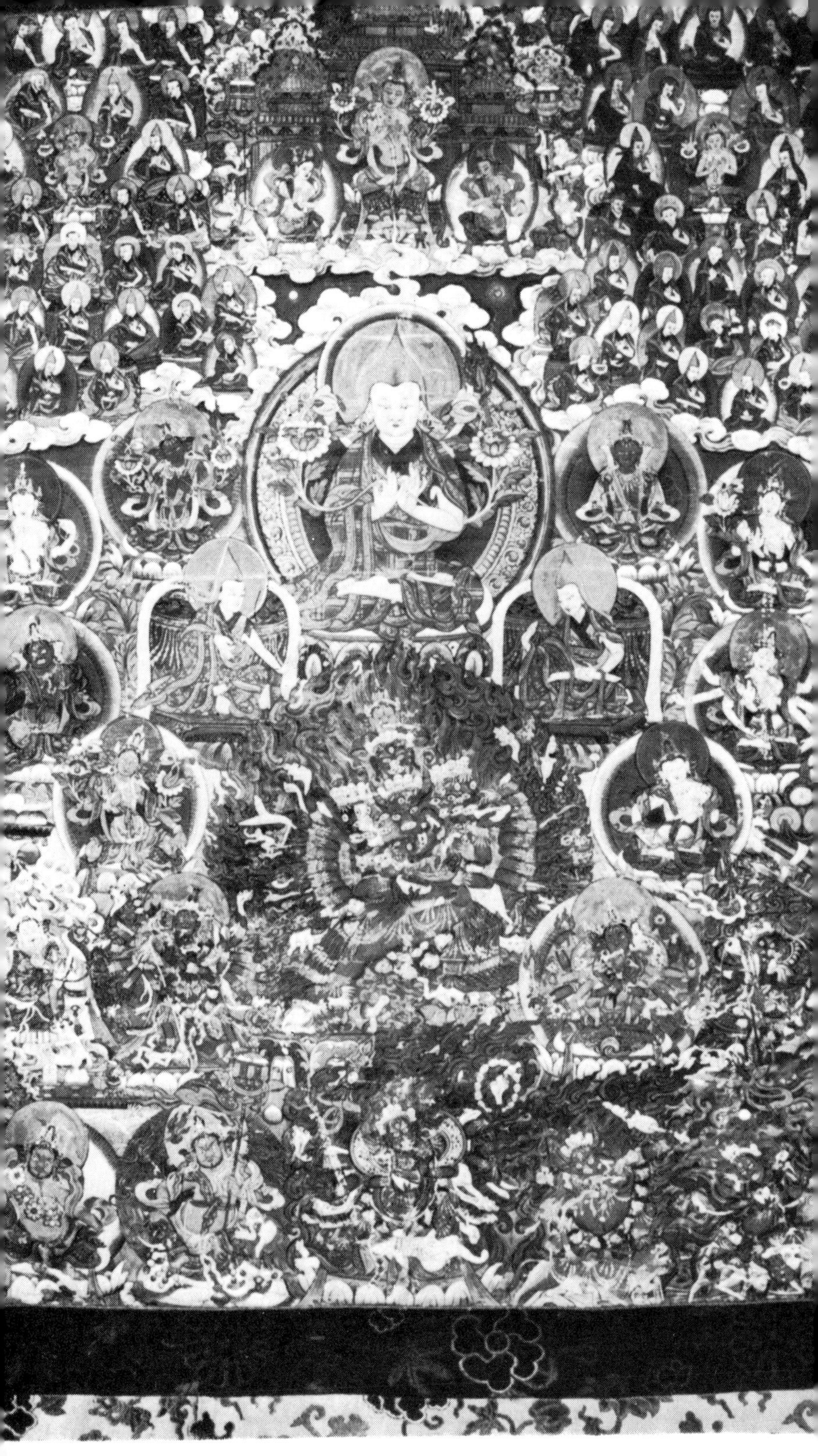

Rays of ten colors: indigo, gold, red, white, wild and dazzling, emanating from the body of the instructor while he was contemplating the abstract and subtle Law, in his omniscience.... The indigo rays coming from his hair and from the blue parts of his eyes. The surface of the sky seemed sprinkled with eye drops, or covered with blue lotus flowers, or even like a fan covered with jewels and fluttering, or a piece of dark fabric completely spread out. The golden rays were shooting out from his skin and from the golden parts of his eyes. From this, the different parts of the globe were sparkling as though sprinkled with a golden liquid, or covered by golden leaves, or sprinkled with saffron and bauhinia flowers. The red rays were coming out of his flesh and blood, as well as the red parts of his eyes. So the four quarters of the globe were colored in red as if with a vermilion powder.... The white rays were emanating from his bones and from his teeth, like the white parts of his eyes, so that the four quarters of the globe were shining, as if washed in floods of milk poured out by silver pots, or covered with a canopy made of silver plaques. . . . The wild and dazzling rays were coming from the different parts of his body. Thus, sprung the six-colored rays which enveloped the great mass of the earth.

\* \* \*

\* \*

\*

# CONTEMPLATIVE TECHNIQUES OF VAJRAYANA

## VAJRAYANA OR THE WAY OF TANTRICISM

Vajrayana is the direct esoteric way that allows the human being who lives in the dark age, or *kali-yuga*, to realize the fusion of his being with the fundamental unity of the Cosmic Whole, in emptiness.

The dark age is the last period, the last cycle of the loss of the original doctrine, the Dharma. According to the followers of Vajrayana, during this age, practices based only on the methods of spiritual realization, are no longer sufficient to lead man to deliverance.

In order for someone to effectively realize the doctrine, he must refer to the four classes of Tantra. In order to attain emptiness, this discipline proposes an ensemble of techniques which are new in terms of the other schools; these include, among others, the practice of visualized mandalas, mantras, and mudras.

We are more closely attached to our body than in preceding ages, and it is through the body that we must seek deliverance. The direct road of perception is no longer accessible to us. The black goddess Kali expands her power over the world, and the dark forces possess man more than ever. In order to free ourselves from them, we have to resort to the perfect knowledge of the physical energies that we possess and that will serve as a vehicle for the spirit so that it may free itself from darkness. The body and the mind, decoded in their depths by an extremely rich symbolic technique, become the testing ground of Illumination.

In its methods, Tantricism relies primarily on the effective realization of its teachings. It is not a question of getting involved in argumentative dialectics, but rather of involving one's whole being in a universe where everything is done to lead the spirit

through a very difficult and arduous road to Illumination. Therefore, the master holds a place of first importance. He is the one
who, through initiation and teachings, prevents the loss of the
soul in its journey. His importance is absolute; he is the true divinity in Vajrayana.

## THE MASTER IN VAJRAYANA

The life of Milarepa gave a particularly precious view of the master–disciple relationship. In quoting the twenty-five precepts of
Vajrayana, which define the duties of the disciple, we will attempt
to give an idea of this special discipline.

1. Respect your Guru.
2. Show proof of your devotion to your Guru in offering him all
that he wants, all that is precious, even the being or the thing you
love above all.
3. Never walk on your Guru's shadow. It is a mistake that is tan-
tamount to the destruction of a temple.
4. Do not step over your Guru's mat or any object that belongs
to him.
5. Whatever your Guru may ask, do it. If you do not understand
one of his directives, ask questions.
6. You must serve your Guru in such a way as if your own life
depended on it.
7. You must serve your Guru's family as if it were your own.
8. In front of your Guru, always take off your hat, and do not
hide your face. Do not remain on a horse in front of him; do not
cross your legs, or make any movements with your arms. If you are
sitting, get up.
9. When your Guru tells you to sit down, sit in a perfect position, as if to meditate. When your Guru gets up, get up also.
10. When your Guru goes for a walk, do not follow him, but
walk at his side. Your clothes and attitude must be simple.
11. When your Guru takes a dangerous path, ask to precede
him.
12. Do not show any sign of fatigue in the presence of your
Guru. Do not lean in order to rest. If you want to take a bath or
wash yourself, ask permission to do so and then remove yourself
from his sight.
13. Always pronounce the name of your Guru in full.

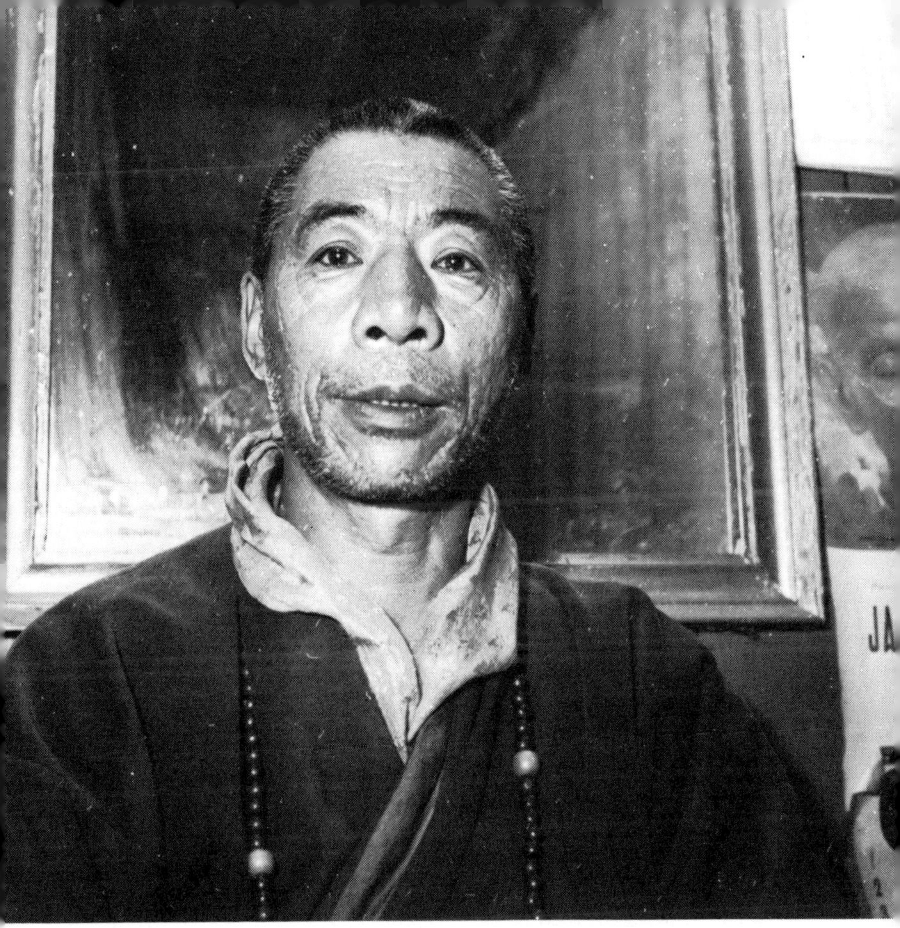

14. Never forget what your Guru has asked you to do.

15. You must not yawn or cough in front of your Guru.

16. When you are speaking to your Guru, bow down before him.

17. If you are a woman, you must not be proud, but possess a simple attitude like a young bride. Bow before him with devotion. Do not lust after his vestments or clothes.

18. You should always consider the perfection of your Guru without noticing his smallest error.

19. When one of the faithful invites you to a meal or a ceremony, get permission from your Guru before going. Whatever you receive as a present, give it as a gift to your Guru. If he gives it back to you, accept it and thank him.

20. Do not take as a disciple any of your Guru's disciples. Never receive any greetings from one of your disciples before he greets your Guru.

21. When you make an offering to your Guru, make it with two hands. And when you receive his blessing, advance your head towards his hands.

22. During the practice of the Dharma, always think of your Guru. If your companions are not serving your Guru faithfully, inform them that their conduct is wrong.

23. If you are sick, ask your Guru for permission to leave your work before you go.

24. You must always make your Guru happy, and serve him attentively.

25. When several Gurus are gathered for a ceremony, and you wish to present them with some offerings, first go to those who occupy the lowest seats.


## THE PANTHEON OF DIVINITIES

One of the essential tasks of the master is the choice of the tutelary divinity of his disciple. After a more or less difficult and lengthy period of test, the Guru confers the initiation on his disciple and has him penetrate the symbolic universe of the chosen divinity. There are several hundred divinities or forms of mandalas. Each one of them portrays a particular aspect of wisdom, and each one of them can lead to final deliverance with no other practice being necessary.

The mandala simultaneously represents the most complete and most perfect symbolic form since it is at the same time a representation of the universe, the body, the mind and the ultimate emptiness. The mandala also represents the hidden place where the noninitiated cannot penetrate and the ideal interior place where the realization of emptiness will take place. Through a process that we will soon describe in detail, the meditator transforms his body into the body of his tutelary divinity. Then, experiencing in his flesh the illusion of all creation, he disolves all form and remains in emptiness.

During the initiation, the master transmits to his disciple the text that must support his meditation and that describes the iconography of the demonic or peaceful divinity that will be seen. He also transmits the corresponding mantras and mudras, which alone can bring about the complete fusion of the disciple and the divinity. A painting on canvas called *tanka* will allow the disciple, after a long and attentive contemplation, to create a mental image in three dimensions perfectly duplicating the original. It is only then that he can visualize this divinity and realize the meditative process as soon as the Master has transmited the power to him.

In order to remain in the field of practical realization and avoid abstractions, we will describe a text as it is transmitted during the course of initiation and as it is used later under the direction of the Master. We have chosen one of the most common initiations, the one of Chenrezig, the god of compassion, of which the Dalai-Lama is an incarnation. Compassion, the most complete love, is in fact, the greatest quality; without it contemplative practice would be ineffective.

## THE MEDITATION OF CHENREZIG

### 1. The preparation

Sitting in the perfect lotus position in your cell or in your hermitage, relax the physical and mental processes of your body through the exercise of silent breathing.

Visualize the cosmos and the revolution of numberless worlds. See this light gradually growing as the stars disappear one after another concentrically, until there is nothing left but the earth.

Visualize the earth with its oceans, its forests, its rivers and its mountains. See this light increasing. The earth melts into light, and there is nothing left but the space of your meditation.

Visualize this place in detail. See each blade of grass, each stone, each vibration that travels through the elements. The light increases and everything vanishes. There is nothing left but your cell.

Visualize your cell in detail. The light is increasing, and it disappears. There is only your body floating in space.

### 2. The three shelters

Repeat the following incantation to your Guru and to the three jewels:

With all living beings, I take refuge in my true Guru.
With all living beings, I take refuge in all the Buddhas.
With all living beings, I take refuge in the Dharma.
With all living beings, I take refuge in Illumination with all the sages.

*Note:* This incantation must be repeated until concentration occurs. As soon as concentration appears, you must either stop

## The Mandala

Every creation of a mandala by the meditator begins with the realization of emptiness. Emptiness is the matrix of the mandala, and the meditator returns to it when he dissolves all images in himself. The structures of the mandala and the divinities that live in it do not have their own existence. Coming from emptiness, they always return to it.

The processes of the creation and Illumination of the mandala that culminates in clear Light is described in the meditation devoted to Chenrezig.

The mandala is the privileged place, the axis of the mental and physical universe, where the disciple realizes emptiness. Through creating the proper iconography of each mandala, the meditator experiences the emptiness of all creation, and becomes, in his turn, the creator of all things. If the mandala is a privileged place, it is because its structure is a double dividing line. It separates the disciple from any intrusion and purifies him by fire of any tie to the world of phenomena.

## The Structure of the Mandala

Going from the periphery to the center, the mandala is constructed as follows:

1. The first circle symbolizes the flames of the five different colors. This barrier of fire prevents the noninitiates from penetrating into the interior of the mandala. It equally destroys all the impurities, all the mental and physical formations of the one who advances to the heart of the mandala where the divinities reside.

2. The second circle symbolizes, through the presence of *vajra*, the ritual tool that forms, with the bell, the unity of Illumination. This is the Circle of the Diamond that gives the disciple the illuminating force, which leads him to emptiness as he penetrates to the heart of the mandala; and there he becomes a divinity himself.

3. The third circle, proper to the mandala representing the angry divinities, is that of eight cemeteries that symbolize the eight forms of consciousness: smell, sight, touch, hearing, taste, intelligence, individual consciousness, and omniscience. Passing through this third circle, the meditator gives up all perceptions, and all consciousness in general that is attached to the world of phenomena.

4. The fourth circle, that of the lotus crown, symbolizes the musical development of all the illuminating forces that lead to the realization of emptiness. It symbolizes the absolute purity of consciousness. Once these four gates are cleared, the disciple is in the very presence of the mandala that floats in the center of pure space.

5. The palace in which the divinities reside is symbolized by the squared quandrangular construction, with four doors guarded by dragons. Around the walls, one often sees

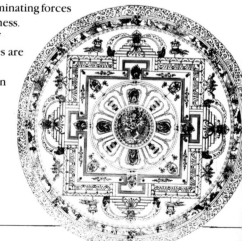

representations of the eight beneficial signs that guarantee success to the spirit that enters the heart of the building.

6. The so-called heart of the mandala is where the disciple's tutelary divinity, which was chosen by the Guru during initiation, resides.

## The Three-Dimensional Mandala

Often, mandala are built in three dimensions. Every detail of the mandala is then constructed in wood, and the divinities are placed in the mandala during the ceremony, in the form of wooden or metal statuettes. The symbolism of each part is identical to the graphic representation.

During my stay in the monastery of Kalo Rinpoche, I was present during the long construction of the mandala photographed here. Each monk participated in it, carving the wood, painting the designs, or modeling the pictures of dragons that were the guardians of the doors and the divinities. When everything was completed according to the instructions of the Master, a great ceremony took place that also marked the departure of many monks from their cells who had isolated themselves for triennial periods of up to twelve years.

the incantation or continue to concentrate simultaneously if it is possible. Having eliminated all external techniques in this meditation, it is very important to understand that no other practice is necessary to reach Illumination.

## 3. The development of the heart of the Bodhi

Repeat three times the following hymn on the heart of the Bodhi:

I will worship the three sacred jewels: the Buddha, the Dharma and the Sages, until I obtain the final fruit of Illumination. With all the good actions I have done or that I will do, may I suddenly become Illuminated.

*Note:* This hymn has to be repeated very slowly, with a melodious voice and with a profound devotion. The compassion and the determination have to be immeasurable. It is from the fruit of the simultaneous development of love and wisdom that Illumination will be born.

## 4. The observance of the six precepts

Repeat three times the following resolution:

I feel compassion for all, and I practice the six precepts:

— Charity
— Morality
— Patience
— Effort
— Meditation
— Wisdom

I meditate so that each may reach the state of Buddha. Charity and compassion for all living beings.

*Note:* Only the observance of precepts and self-denial can guarantee a fruitful meditation. The greater the renunciation of the things of this world, the faster will be the improvement in vision and accomplishment.

## 5. The four openings of the Spirit

Repeat the following sentences with the most profound concentration:

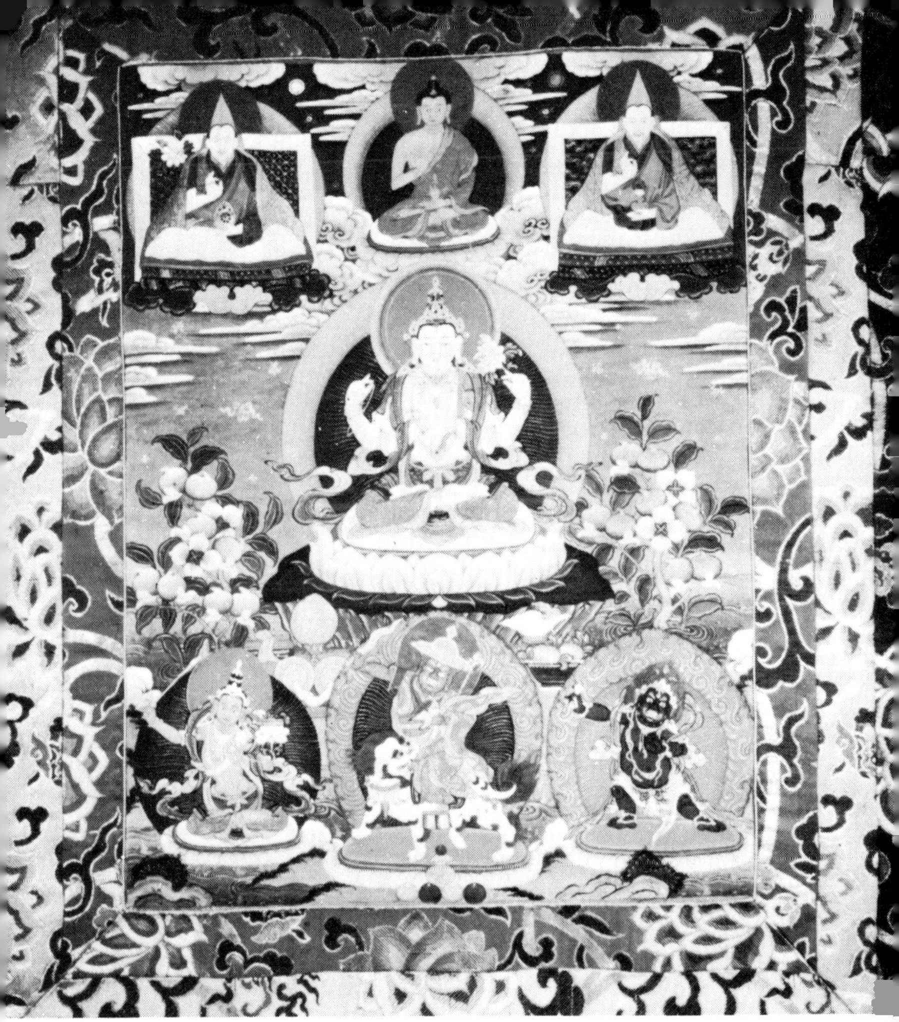

*Chenrezig, the Bodhisattva of compassion, whose complete text of meditation is given here.*

May all living beings possess joy and its fruits.

May all living beings free themselves from suffering and its causes.

May all living beings experience spiritual bliss.

May all living beings free themselves from attachment and hatred and remain in Equanimity.

*Note:* Let your soul be full of understanding of the law of causality. When you are moved by the consciousness of the suffering of the world, let every concept flow out of your soul. In internal silence and in the peace of the spirit, wait for the luminous rising of concentration for as long as it takes before going to the next stage.

## 6. *The birth of the lotus and of the letter*

Visualize the following manifestations:

A lotus appears above your head, positioned at the top of your skull. Above it, floating in space and illuminated by the full moon that is the size of your body and that is behind you, the letter 𑀽, blue in color, radiates through the ten directions of empty space.

*Note:* It is important that this vision be extremely luminous and translucent before going on. Rushing would result in tarnishing the rest of the meditation. It is necessary to wait as long as it takes for each element to be seen with great clarity.

## 7. *The apparition of Chenrezig*

Visualize the following manifestations:

With the suddenness of a rainbow that appears, the letter changes into Chenrezig's body. The body is extremely luminous, and the diaphanous skin shines brightly in empty space. The five colors: red, white, blue, yellow, and green radiate from the different parts of the body. The face is of a greaty beauty and it smiles. The eyes remain fixed on your body. Two of the hands are joined in front of the chest, and in the mudra of emptiness, they are holding a precious treasure. The two other hands are unfolded on each side of the body. The figure is holding a lotus in the left hand and a rosary of 108 beads in the right hand. He is wearing beautiful red silk clothes, and his body is ornamented with glittering jewels. An animal skin covers his left breast and on his crown, which shines of a thousand fires, is the red-colored Amitabha, symbol of accomplished wisdom, sitting in the lotus position. Behind Chenrezig shines an immaculate full moon.

I am meditating so that the entire universe may be liberated from suffering and from the cycle of rebirths. The whole universe takes refuge in the body of Chenrezig. The divinity and my precious Guru form one and the same person.

*Note:* It is very important that the divinity be visualized with all its attributes, its different colors and the light that comes from it. The tanka, placed in front of the meditator, can be used to dispel the haziness that sometimes replaces certain parts of the body when concentration is displaced at a precise point.

## 8. *The vision of the progeny of the Guru*

Visualize the following manifestations:

Above Amitabha's red-colored body, visualize the body of your own Guru, and above him, ascending into space, the bodies of the Gurus who are his spiritual lineage.

In the same way, you will see that above your own Guru is Milarepa, light blue in color, right hand laid against his cheek and left hand on his knee, holding a skull full of nectar, his body clothed in white silk.

Above him stands Marpa. His skin is dark and his body shows a powerful bulk. He is wearing the gown of lamas. His hands are holding a skull full of nectar.

Above him stands Naropa, light blue in color. His hair is gathered above his head and it is very long. He is wearing a crown of human skulls, and his right hand is holding a horn made out of an antelope's antler, while his left hand is making a menacing mudra and his feet are in the position of a blacksmith.

Above him is Tilopa, brown in color, with his hair held up. He is wearing a white lotus tiara and a meditation belt. His body is covered with a tiger skin. His right hand is holding a golden fish, and his left hand, a skull full of nectar.

Above him is the divinity Vajra-Dhara, blue in color. He is holding the bell and the diamond sceptre.

Having a clear sight of the progeny of Gurus, may your heart be filled with devotion. With great emotion, then say the prayer of the progeny and implore the waves of beneficence that will allow you to realize emptiness.

'Pour out your waves of beneficence, O Guru, and grant me the Four Powers.

Pour out your waves of beneficence, so that everything in the universe assumes the characteristics of the divinity.

Pour out your waves of beneficence, so that I can transform my body into a Divine One.

Pour out your waves of beneficence, so that I can dissolve the illusion.

Pour out your waves of beneficence, so that I can see the profound Emptiness in myself.

Pour out your waves of beneficence, so that I can reach in this very life the state of Buddha.'

When you have addressed this prayer to the progeny of Gurus, concentrate on them, and in a brighter and brighter light, see their dissolution in your own Guru. Then repeat the prayer to your Guru alone, who has the powers of the whole progeny. With an intense fervor, implore his waves of beneficence and the transfer of his psychic strength into you. Then, in a very bright light, reabsorb the image of your Guru into that of Amitabha and then into that of Chenrezig.

*Note:* This entire visualization must be extremely clear. It is necessary to contemplate for a long time on the tankas showing Milarepa, Marpa, Naropa, Tilopa and Vajra-Dhara so as to mentally recreate them without forgetting the least detail.

## 9. The transformation of the body into the divinity

Visualize the following manifestations:

The body of Chenrezig is becoming luminous and generating heat. Its light is diffused in all of space. The impurity and the ignorance that are still in your body are being dissipated. You are becoming clear and pure. Totally absorbed by the contemplation of the divinity, your body slowly opens itself to light that goes through you like hot lava. Gradually, as the light penetrates your body, you become the divinity, with its attributes. You are Chenrezig. Your light illuminates the entire universe, all the impurities and stains of the universe are dissolved by the force of light. Everything is clarity, divine purity.

*Note:* The transformation of the body of the meditator into the body of the divinity has to be accomplished very slowly and must abolish any consciousness of the past form of the meditator.

## 10. The mantra

Visualize the following manifestations:

In your divine body, a six-petal lotus suddenly appears at the level of the heart. The full moon that is behind you shines through your divine body. The letter 𐐸 appears above the lotus, it is blue.

Then begin to say the mantra by concentrating, one after the other, on each of the petals of the open lotus, which represent the six segments of the mantra:

### Om Mani Padme Hum

*Note:* The mantra has to be repeated a great number of times in the same way that the Guru taught it during the course of the initiation. The rosary, which sometimes is used to count the mantra, possesses 108 beads. It is common to complete the string a number of times. Through repeating the mantras, the strength of concentration increases little by little, and the luminosity of the divine body becomes so bright that the thinker acknowledges an ecstatic joy allowing him to go to the next stages.

## 11. The dissolution of the divine body

Visualize the following manifestations:

The light of your divine body spreads into the world and illuminates it. Then, it returns into your body and illuminates it with the suddenness of the rainbow, afterwards dissolving into space. All that is left is the letter in empty space. An extremely bright light illuminates it.

*Note:* The energy and the illuminating force that reside in the body of the divinity must, after its illumination and fusion in space, find itself again in the letter, and its blue color must be very intense.

## 12. The Fusion into emptiness

Visualize the following manifestations:

Concentrate on the letter.

An extremely bright light illuminates  ৺ , which disappears.

An extremely bright light illuminates  ২ , which disappears.

An extremely bright light illuminates  ৯ , which disappears.

An extremely bright light illuminates  ৹ , which disappears.

Remain in the emptiness for as long as possible.

*Note:* The last disappearance brings forth the final ecstasy, which is the entire disappearance of the Self in emptiness. Perceptions melt into space, leaving room for the final state that words cannot describe.

The more we speak and the more we speculate, the more we separate from the Way. If we omit all speech and all reflection, there is no place where we cannot go.

Things in themselves do not know distinctions: the latter are born from our attachment. To put your mind to your own uses, isn't this the worst of all errors?

Everything is empty, shining and luminous by itself: Do not overwork your spiritual strengths! The absolute is not a place that can be measured by thought and knowledge cannot explore it.

*Hsin-Hsin-Ming*[1]

\*   \*   \*
\*   \*
\*

# CONTEMPLATIVE TECHNIQUES OF CH'AN (ZEN)

## THE CHARACTERISTICS OF THE CH'AN, OR ZEN, SCHOOL

The best way to comprehend the different aspects of Zen and to attempt an approach to it is undoubtedly to live in the utmost simplicity. Zen is different from the other Buddhist schools in four essential ways, that will be examined in the following order:

1. Special transmission beyond what is told in the Scriptures.
2. Do not rely on the texts.
3. Reveal directly to each man his original mind.
4. Contemplate your own nature in order to obtain the state of the Buddha.

### 1. Special transmission beyond what is told in the scriptures

In the school of Zen, the traditional scriptures of the Buddha are not considered to be a means of reaching Illumination. In fact, this type of Illumination can only be sudden and outside of all cultural bounds.

In Zen there is no veneration for the ancient texts, and one can even say that they are considered as obstacles to the final realization.

The master is then seen as a living doctrine, or rather as the non-doctrine. The disciple does not approach the master in order to get any verbal teaching. This would endlessly allude to particular sutras, which are intended to open up the soul of the disciple by a series of references.

The Zen master does not believe that he can infuse his disciple with what he himself has realized by way of scriptures or by way of direct teaching. He does not seek to create a progressive state of understanding. Instead he waits with a faithful and penetrating attention for the moment when he will be able to rend by a sharp blow the illusory film that still separates the disciple from the realization of his own nature, which has always been that of the Buddha.

The Zen master is searching for any method that will short-circuit the mental associations and intellectual creations of his disciples, so that one day Illumination will fill them with the suddenness of lightning. For this delicate operation, the tradition of Zen always associates itself with the most direct and simplest methods. A word, a gesture, an attitude or a violent blow will sometimes suffice to let the bottom fall out and open the mind to Illumination.

The art of the master rests wholly on the choice of the means best-adapted to the personality of his disciple, and above all, on the choice of the most sudden means.

The literature of Zen describes different series of precise actions that have led to the awakening of particular disciples. When the impasse into which the master leads his disciple is sufficiently abrupt and sudden, all the circuits of thought are abandoned, and the disciple experiences awakening.

One asks: What was the idea of Bodhidharma's coming to the west?

The Master answers: If he had had an idea, he would not even have succeeded in saving himself.

They say: If he had no idea, how could the Second Patriarch have obtained the law?

The Master says: To obtain is not to obtain.

They say: If there is no obtaining, what is the idea of non-obtainment?

The Master says: Because you are pursuing, looking all over, and unable to quiet your mind that the Master Patriarch said: Fie! The jovial fellow, who with his head, is looking for his head!

Learn to see things according to these words. Stop looking! Know that, in body or in mind, you are not different from the Patriarch Buddha, and very soon you will be trouble free: it is this alone that is called obtaining the Law.[1]

Hui-k'o unceasingly interrogated Bodhidharma, begging him to instruct him: he kept being refused. Nevertheless, he persisted in sitting, meditating in front of his cell, waiting patiently in the snow for Bodhidharma to agree finally to yield. Desperate one day, Hui-k'o cut off his left arm and showed it to Bodhidharma as testimony of his sincerity.

As last Bodhidharma asked Hui-k'o what he desired.
 – I have no peace of mind, pacify my mind, I beg you!
 – Bring your mind here in front of me and I will pacify it!
 – But when I look for it, I can't find it.
 – That's it! I have pacified your mind.
 At that very moment, Hui-k'o achieved awakening.

What is the method of deliverance, Tao-hsin asked?
Who is enslaving you? Seng-ts'an asked.
No one is enslaving me.
Then why are you looking for deliverance?
At this moment, Tao-hsin awakened.

A monk asked Ch'ao-chou:
 – I just entered your monastery. Teach me, Master.
 – Have you eaten your rice?
 – Yes.
 – Then go and wash your bowl.
 At that instant, the monk awakened.

## 2. Don't rely on the texts

Thought is pure by nature, and all mental construction tarnishes it. All search ends up contrary to its goal. By their detachment from texts, the Zen Masters intend to force their disciples not to dwell any longer in sterile erudition and to turn away from language in order to free the mind from any impurity. They also condemn strict attachment to law, and even the attachment to notions of emptiness, search and Illumination. In this way, they point directly to intuition.

The seeds of the Buddha, hidden in my spirit, will blossom when the penetrating rain comes.
The flower of the Doctrine, having been intuitively seized,
The fruit of Illumination will necessarily be picked.[2]

Lin-chi adopts a much more caustic position: 'There are those people who ignore good and evil and utilize speculations and discussions on the teaching, making sentence-by-sentence commentaries on them. It is as if they were putting pieces of shit into their mouths and spitting them out again in order to transmit them to others.'[3]

In the collection *Entering Without a Door*, there is the following poem:

Language does not develop the fact.
The word does not coincide with living movement.
He who accepts the word loses himself.
He who stagnates in the word strays.[4]


## *3. Reveal directly to each man his original mind*

There exists a Chinese poem on jade which, applied to the mind, gives an altogether Zenlike idea of its nature:

There exists in the world a marvelous thing,
Very precious, simple and without ornamentation.
Carve it for a vulgar usage.
In an instant, its purity is altered. . . .[5]

Like jade, the mind must be left in total freedom, and any attempt to use it for obtaining supreme knowledge leads to darkness.

Therefore, Zen has as objective the realization of the immaculate and fundamental purity of one's mind. This wisdom, this absolute purity, is the very nature of the Buddha, which the master reveals to his disciple without bringing in any element that could contribute to the darkening of its original nature.

That your mind may be in a state like that of unlimited emptiness, but not attached to the idea of emptiness, so that it acts freely! Whether in activity or at rest, do not stop your mind anywhere. Forget the difference between the wise and the ordinary man. Ignore all distinctions between subject and object. Leave your own nature as well as all phenomenal objects in the state of Identity. Then, you will always be in the state of supreme concentration (samadhi).[6]


## *4. Contemplate your own nature in order to obtain the state of the Buddha*

Every outwardly directed search is a waste of time and energy. The state of the Buddha is obtained neither by knowledge nor by rites. There is no method, properly speaking, and no goal. The only thing that distinguishes the ordinary man and the illuminated man is that the former has not realized the pure and fundamental nature in himself.

Adepts, if you wish to conform to the Law, guard only against doubt. In your outwardness you will embrace the whole plan of things, and in your inwardness there will not be anything more to establish, even to the measure of a silk thread, or a strand of hair. What do you call this so distinct thing, this solitary light in which nothing was ever lacking, but which the eye does not see, and the ear does not hear? An Ancient said: To say that this is a thing is to miss the target.

Look inside yourself! What more is there?
Talking about it could go on forever.
Let everyone strive!
Salute![7]

## THE PURIFICATION OF THOUGHT

If Zen believes in sudden Illumination, it still does not reject all inner work. The action that each of us can undertake alone does not constitute progressive Illumination up to the final deliverance, but rather a purification of internal ground so that awakening can take place suddenly in its integrality. Lin-chi, a fierce opponent of methods, used to say:

One must still experiment personally to be purified like a mineral, to be polished like a bronze mirror: then, one fine morning, you wake up.[8]

The Sixth Patriarch recommends this purification as well.

What we need to do is to purify our thought, so that the six agents of consciousness belonging to sight, hearing, smell, taste, touch, and mind, in passing through the six doors, are not corrupted and do not tie themselves to the six objects of the senses.

When our spirit works unhindered and is free to go and come, we reach the samadhi of Wisdom, which rescues us and sets us free; this is the application of non-attachment.[9]

## THE SITTING MEDITATION, ZAZEN

Although a great number of Zen masters strongly rejected the practice of Zazen because they felt it was an illusory activity and a creator of activity and darkness, other masters gave it priority as an exercise.
  Here is what Lin-chi said on this subject:

There are bald, sightless individuals who, after having eaten their fill of grain, sit in Dhyana in order to devote themselves to the contemplative exercises. They grasp all the impurities of thought while attempting to control thought; they are looking for silence because they detest noise. These are heretical procedures. A patriarchal master has said: Fix the mind on considering silence, reinstate it to examine the external world, regather it to make it flow, and solidify it to enter into concentration.

All this is merely makeshift work. As for you, you who are there, listening to the Law, how could you wish to cultivate fruits of culture and act in such a way? Why do you want to embellish yourself? You are not meant to be cultivated, to be embellished; if you are, then all beings can be embellished. Stop fooling yourselves![10]

The Sixth Patriarch seemed to share this opinion:

A living man sits
and does not lie down forever,
While a dead man
stays stretched out and does not sit.

Why do we impose on our bodies the physical pain of the meditation posture?[11]

The Adepts of Zazen practice a special posture that has the following essential characteristics:

Sitting on the *zafu* (round cushion), legs crossed in the lotus or half-lotus position, one pushes against the ground with the knees and against the sky with the head; the spinal column is arched, the pelvis tilted forward, at the level of the fifth lumbar; the abdomen completely relaxed, the neck straight, and the chin pulled in. One is like a stretched bow whose arrow is the mind. Sitting in this posture, without goal or desire of gain, keep the eyes fixed three feet in front of you; the eyes look at nothing. The left hand is placed in the right hand with the palms upwards, and the thumbs are joined like the horizon, 'neither mountain nor valley', the shoulders falling naturally and the tip of the tongue against the palate: this is the posture. Breathing plays a primordial role. When concentrating on the longest possible exhalation, while the attention is focused on posture, inhalation comes naturally.

The idea-images that pass through the mind and the unconscious thoughts that arise must not be stopped or maintained during Zazen.[12]

During meditation, the master comes and goes, holding a *kyōsaku*, a long stick with a flat end. It is used both to wake up those who are asleep with a violent blow on the shoulders and to massage the shoulders and the back, in order to release them into the correct position and adjust the mind. Sometimes, when the stick is wielded by a great master, its blows also permit the disciple to experience sudden awakening, as many Zen texts have informed us.

Zazen is regularly interrupted by rhythmical walking, by manual labor, and by meals.

For the adepts of Zen, to meditate means to realize the fundamental emptiness of one's own nature. It is a deliverance that leads simply to seeing things the way they really are, in their most naked reality. Meditation can lead anyone to awakening. There is no cultural discrimination in Zen. The Sixth Patriarch himself was illiterate.

Here is the definition of meditation that Huai-hai gives:

> When the flux of thought stops, there is meditation. If you remain motionless in the contemplation of your real nature, you are in samadhi. For in truth, your original nature is the eternal spirit. In samadhi, your soul pulls back from things that surround you; it could not even be moved by the Eight Winds, which are profit, loss, calumny, praise, flattery, mockery, sadness, and joy. If you can concentrate in this manner, no matter how ordinary you are, you will enter Buddhahood.[13]

## PHYSICAL WORK

If not all Zen masters agree on the necessity of sitting meditation, they all do see manual work as a precious tool of liberation.

There are many anecdotes in Zen literature that describe masters who assign over-contemplative disciples the most menial tasks. The Sixth Patriarch himself was told this by his master.

'This man has too much wind. Go back to the stable and don't speak any more.'

The Zen Master, Pai-ch'ang established the tradition of physical work with this famous maxim:

'He who does not work does not eat.'

Each task is accepted by the monk as a noble action that elevates man. No discrimination is involved. Everything is accomplished with equality so as to remain as far as possible from intellectual speculations, which are the greatest enemy of Zen. All absence from the physical reality of life corresponds to a loss of original purity and all commentary tarnishes the profound nature of man.

'An idle dream is not our affair,' Zen adepts say.

Ideas that do not express an immediate and concrete realiza-

*Having come from China where archery was considered an ascetic exercise by the Taoists, this art found in Zen its supreme flowering. One day, in a sudden and unexpected way, the archer will accomplish the spontaneous act that is detached from every form of thought. Not until*

*that day will be be an archer. It may require an entire life of daily exercise, and a constant surpassing of the ego in order to realize a total fusion with the universe, the perfect gesture.*

tion are totally valueless, and logic is acceptable only to the extent that it is expressed by a noble and disinterested act.

## BEING A SIMPLE MAN

The whole practice of Zen is directed toward being a simple man who does his ordinary jobs, stays away from intellectual practices and considers life and his own nature as they are, that is to say, stripped of every reality and therefore empty. This man then realizes that he is the Buddha, and all search comes to nothing. To those who are thirsty for theory, Lin-chi replies:

Adepts, there is no work in Buddhism. It is all a matter of remaining simple, and acting without a fuss.

To shit and to piss, to get dressed and to eat.
When tiredness comes, I sleep;
The fools laugh at me, the wise know me.
An elder said:
Only the imbeciles do external work.[14]

Be your own Master wherever you are, and at once, you will be true.

## THE ONE HUNDRED AND TWELVE WAYS OF MEDITATION

In order to fully understand the fundamental spirit of the individual who devotes himself to contemplation and dissolves his being in an ecstasy in which all mental differences are extinguished, we will now present the One Hundred Twelve Precepts. All these precepts are known under one form or another by all the Tibetan, Hindu, and Chinese monks who devote themselves to contemplation. These texts, which were transmitted to me by a Chinese yogi, who was a refugee in India, are virtually unknown in the West. Nevertheless, they describe very precisely the profound sense of the spiritual and physical attitude of the individual who lives in search of the nameless light.

C. M. Chen, after having lived as a recluse in a Himalayan cave, established himself in a hermitage. Since 1947, he has lived there without ever leaving his retreat. In continuous meditation, he contemplates the light of knowledge. He has classified the precepts of Zen and Shiva, the One Hundred Twelve Ways of meditation, into twelve categories, each of which concerns a particular aspect of the ascetic way.

Some of these precepts have a hidden aspect, and their meaning seems difficult to penetrate. This is part of the Zen tradition, which requires a great concentration in order to understand intuitively and not intellectually. After a few seconds of concentration, words suddenly enlighten from within, and the realization that is provoked touches the being in depth.

## THE NINE FIRST PRECEPTS CONCERNING BREATHING

1. This experience must occur between two breaths. When the air goes into the lungs, and just before it comes out, *experience its vitality*.

2. Between the inhalation and the exhalation and between the exhalation and the inhalation, as the breath shifts, from bottom to top and from top to bottom, *realize* through this movement.

3. At the time of exhalation and inhalation, at this precise instant, meet the *center of energy* without wasting any strength.

4. When you have completely breathed out or in, and the movement stops by itself, in that universal position, the *idea of Self disappears*. This is difficult only for those who are impure.

5. Focus attention between the two eyebrows, and keep your mind free from all thought. Let your form be filled with the essence of breathing to the top of the head, and there, *bathe in the light*.

6. When you devote yourself to worldly activities, focus your attention between the two movements of breathing and thus, in a few days, *you will be born again*.

7. Arrive at an intangible breathing concentrated in the middle of the forehead. When it arrives at the heart, just before sleep, master your dreams and *death itself*.

8. With the utmost devotion, concentrate on the junctions of breathing and *penetrate he who knows*.

9. Rest as if dead, or full of anger. Remain like that or look without moving an eyelash; or suck on something and *become what you are sucking*.

## ELEVEN WAYS CONCERNING LETTERS
## AND THEIR SOUNDS

1. Imagine the Sanskrit letters, be filled with honey and keep your consciousness empty. Visualize, at first, the letters. Then, more subtly, the sounds. Finally a subtle and undefined feeling. Discard it and *be free*.

2. Enter the center of sound as if you were present in the continuous sound of a small waterfall. Or, while putting your fingers into your ears, hear *the sound of sounds*.

3. Chant a sound like AUM slowly. Enter into the sound while AUM *glides into the sonorous state*.

4. At the beginning of the gradual refinement of a sound, *wake up*.

5. When you are listening to string instruments, hear the *central omnipresent sound*.

6. Sing a tone clearly, slower and slower until the presence of silence occurs. Knowledge comes from this *silent harmony*.

7. With the mouth slightly open, place your mind in the center of your tongue. When the breath silently penetrates, perceive the sound HH.

8. Concentrate on the sound AUM without perceiving either the A or the M.

9. Silently sing a word ending with AH. Then, in HH, attain *spontaneity*.

10. Stop the perception of sound by closing your ears. By contracting the rectum, enter into sound.

11. Penetrate into the sound of your own name, and through this sound, know *all sounds*.

## TWELVE WAYS CONCERNING THE POINT OR THE CENTER
## OF ZEN MEDITATION

1. Imagine the five colored circles of the peacock's feathers as being the five senses in unlimited space. Now, let their beauty melt into you. Do the same thing on any point in space or on a wall until the spot *disappears*. Then your desire for other things will be realized.

2. Place your attention, delicately, like a petal of a lotus, on the

central nerve, in the middle of the spinal column. Now *be transformed*.

3. Close the seven openings of the head with your hands, and a space between your eyes unites *the all*.

4. Blessed is the one who attains the center of the lotus when the senses have melted into the heart.

5. Mind without mind, dwell in the center.

6. Look lovingly at an object. Do not look at anything else. Here, in the center of this object, lies *happiness*.

7. Without the support of your feet or hands, sit down on your rear end. Suddenly, *concentration*.

8. In a moving vehicle, rocking rhythmically, or in a stopped vehicle, making it move yourself in slow, invisible circles, *experience*.

9. Pierce a spot on your form that is filled with nectar with a pin, and slowly, penetrate inside the hole.

10. Let attention penetrate a place where you see a past event, and your form, having lost its present characteristics, will be transformed.

11. Perceive an object in front of you. Experience the complete absence of everything else. Then, go away from the sensation of the object and the absence of sensation. Now *realize*.

12. When you have an emotion for or against someone, do not put it on the person in question but *remain in its center*.


SEVEN WAYS CONCERNING THE ACTION OF LOOKING


1. Eyes closed, observe your interior being in detail. Then observe your *true nature*.

2. Look at a bowl without considering its sides or what it is made of. Instantly, *seize awareness*.

3. Observe a very beautiful person or an ordinary thing as if for the first time.

4. Find *serenity* simply by looking at the blue sky behind the clouds.

5. Listen when the ultimate mystical teaching has been given. Eyes calm, without blinking, *totally free yourself*.

6. At the well's edge, completely still, feel its depth until you touch your *astonishment*.

7. Look at one object. Then, slowly, remove your glance. Then take away your thought. Then. . .

## THREE WAYS CONCERNING THE SENSATION
## OF NON-POSSESSION OF THE BODY

1. When you caress, enter into the *caress* as if into eternal life.

2. Close the doors of the senses when you feel the tinglings. *Then* . . .

3. When you are in bed or in a chair, let yourself *float in space*.

## NINE WAYS CONCERNING THE LIGHT

1. Consider your essence like rays of light that go from one center to the other along the vertebrae. In the same way, *life* will rise in you.

2. In the meantime, feel *luminous*.

3. Perceive the Cosmos as an eternal *translucent* presence.

4. In summer, when you see the full, clear sky up to infinity, *penetrate into that clarity.*

5. See all of space as if it were absorbed into your own head. *Light.*

6. Walking, sleeping, dreaming, know yourself as *light.*

7. When it is raining on a dark night, penetrate into the *darkness* as the Form of forms.

8. During a rainy, moonless night, close your eyes and find the darkness in front of you. Then, open your eyes and see the *darkness.* In the same way, mistakes will disappear forever.

9. When your attention awakens, at that precise moment, *experience.*

## FIVE WAYS TO ENTER INTO CONCENTRATION
## BY THE PRACTICE OF STOPPING

1. At the precise moment when you have the impulse of doing something, *stop.*

2. When a desire comes, observe it, then *suddenly* abandon it.

3. Wander until exhausted. Then let yourself fall to the ground, and in this fall, *remain complete.*

4. Suppose that you are gradually deprived of energy and knowledge. At the instant of this occurrence, *transcend*.

5. Devotion *frees*.


## TWELVE WAYS CONCERNING THE GREAT FUSION
## OR THE OMNIPRESENCE


1. Touch the eyeballs as if with a feather. Between them the *luminosity opens the heart*, and through there, passes the Cosmos.

2. The friendly Devi comes in. The ethereal presence, it *infiltrates* far above and below your form.

3. Transform the mind into a material of inexpressible fineness and pour it above, below and *into your heart*.

4. Consider all parts of your present form as *unlimited space*.

5. Feel your substance, bones, flesh and blood, filled with *cosmic essence*.

6. Feel the excellent creative qualities filter through your chest and assume *delicate forms*.

7. Remain in an *infinitely spacious* expanse deprived of trees, hills, and dwellings. From that comes the relaxation of the mind.

8. Consider the winds as your own *body of happiness*.

9. In a comfortable lotus position, a zone of emptiness is gradually spreading between the underarms and causing *profound peace*.

10. Feel yourself as if you were *spreading* in all directions, infinitely.

11. The appreciation of objects and beings is the same for an illuminated person as for an ordinary one. The former has an advantage: he remains in a state of mind that does not get lost in things.

12. Believe in the penetration of the *Omniscient*, and the *Omnipotent*.


## TWENTY-ONE WAYS CONCERNING THE PRACTICE OF ZEN
## IN RELATION TO DESIRES AND MENTAL STATES


1. In the *beginning* of sexual union, be attentive to the fire, and continuing this way, avoid the live coals at the end.

2. When you are in such a union, your senses vibrate like leaves in the wind. *Enter into that vibration.*

3. Even when you remember a union, with the embrace, comes *the transformation.*

4. When, full of joy, you meet a friend after a long separation, *allow yourself that joy.*

5. When you eat or drink, become the taste of what you swallow and be *filled* with that taste.

6. You, sweet being of the lotus eye, when you sing, look, taste, be aware that you exist and discover *eternal life.*

7. Even if you find satisfaction in some action, *realize that.*

8. At the moment you go to sleep, when sleep has not yet come, but the state of wakefulness is disappearing, at that precise instant, the fact *of being* will be revealed to you.

9. Illusions deceive. Colors limit, and the divisions are indivisible.

10. In a state of extreme desire, be at peace.

11. What you call the universe is an illusion, a conjuring trick. In order to be happy, consider it *as such.*

12. O beloved, put your attention neither on pleasure nor pain but *between the two of them.*

13. Objects and desires exist in you as in others. Accept them as such and let them *transfer themselves.*

14. Waves come with water and flames come with fire. Similarly the universe trembles *due to the movements of our minds.*

15. When your mind flits externally and internally, at that precise place, *that.*

16. When you are suddenly conscious of a particular feeling, remain as if your consciousness were flying in space, in the thick of things, in a state of extreme curiosity. At the beginning of your hunger and at the most extreme point of your hunger, *always be austere.*

17. The purity of other doctrines is impurity for us. In reality, do not recognize *anything* as pure or impure.

18. *Be the same* for a foreigner or a friend. Remain the same in honor and in dishonor.

19. There is a sphere of change, movement, and mutation. Across these transformations, *consume the movement.*

20. When a hen raises its chicks with knowledge and habits, it does it *in reality.*

21. Truly, slavery and freedom are relative. These words exist

only for those who are terrified by the universe. This universe is the reflection of spirits. As you perceive many suns in the water *coming from the sun*, so in the same manner you perceive slavery and liberty.

## ELEVEN WAYS RELATED TO THE SELF

1. Concentrate on a fire that rises from your feet and consumes you. Your body is in ashes but *you remain*.

2. Meditate on the burning world. Then on its ashes and *transcend the human*.

3. As letters are transformed subjectively into words and words into phrases and sentences, and as circles are transformed objectively into worlds and worlds into elements, find again these convergences *in yourself*.

4. O dearest, meditate on knowledge and the lack of knowledge, the existent and the non-existent. Then put away even *your own existence*.

5. Feel: my thought, my self, my organs, *Me*.

6. Before desiring and before knowing, how can I say: I am. Consider the world, then dissolve yourself in *the beauty*.

7. Reject the attachment to the body in realizing that *you are everywhere*. He who is in everything is joyous.

8. Do not think and the Self will *no longer have limitations*.

9. Suppose that you contemplate something beyond perception, ungraspable, beyond not being, *yourself*.

10. I exist. That belongs to me. That is that. O beloved, even in such states, know the *unlimited*.

11. Beloved, at this moment, leave the mind, learning, breathing, form, and *embrace totality*.

## SEVEN WAYS CONCERNING CONSCIOUSNESS

1. Imagine the mind, simultaneously, in you and around you until the whole universe is *spiritualized*.

2. With your entire consciousness in the very beginning of the desire to know, *realize*.

3. All specific perceptions are limited. Dissolve yourself in the *all powerful*.

4. In truth, forms are not divided. Your omnipresent being and your own form rest in unity. Realize that each one is made of this consciousness.

5. Experience the consciousness of each being as *your own*.

6. This consciousness exists as each being, *and nothing else exists*.

7. This consciousness is the spirit that leads each being. *Be that.*

## THREE WAYS CONCERNING EMPTINESS

1. Go into space, eternally, without stirring.

2. Imagine your shape to be an empty room with walls of skin. *Empty.*

3. Free: to play in the universe is to be a shell within which your spirit flits into infinity.

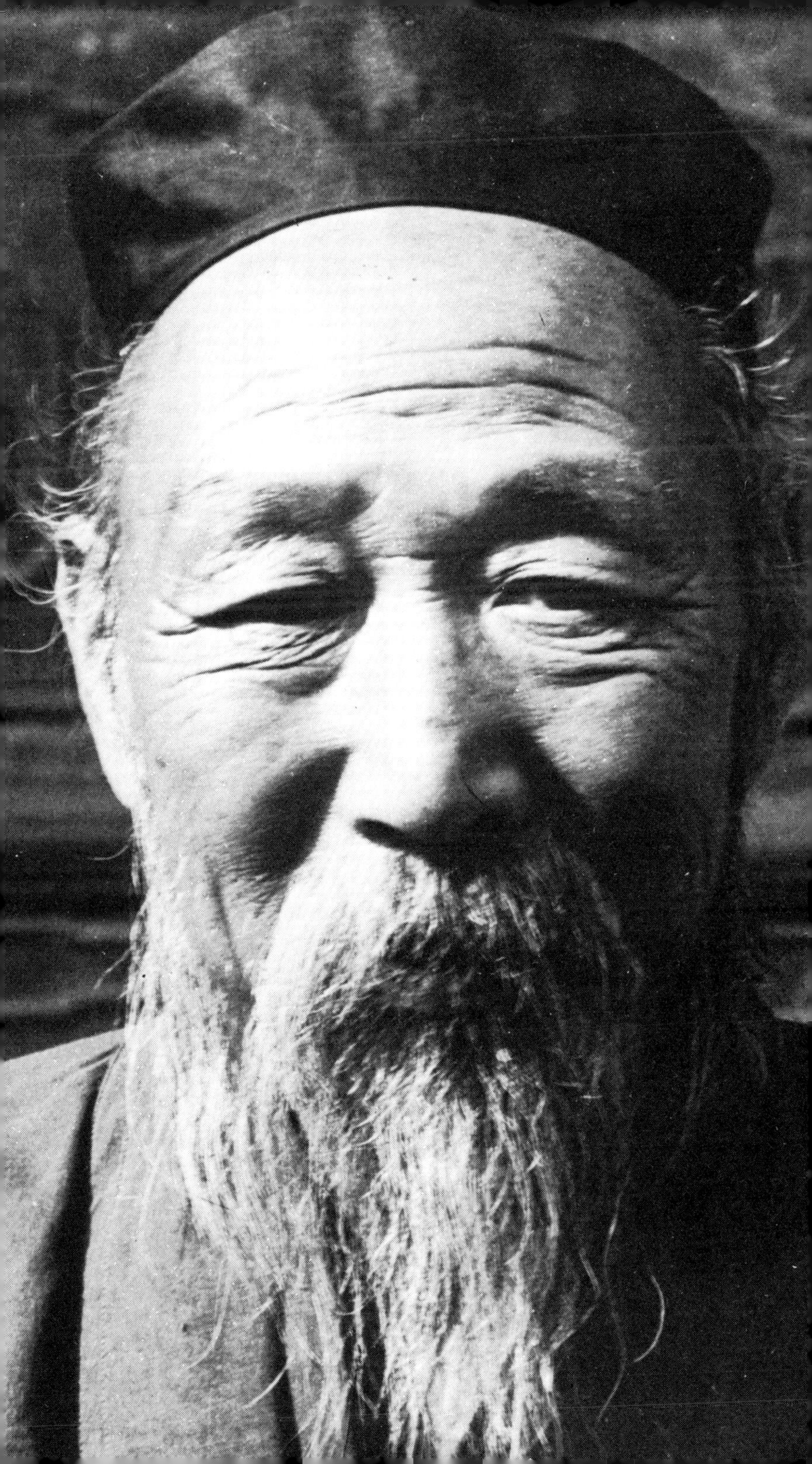

# PART II

\*

# TAOISM

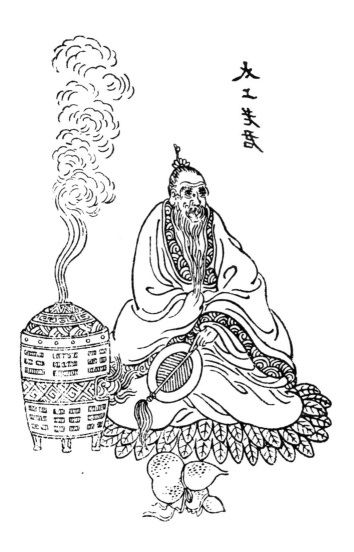

The one who knows does not speak,
the one who speaks does not know.

Cover your opening,
Shut your door,
Take the edge off your blade,
untie all skeins,
blend all lights,
unite all particles,
this is the supreme identity.

You cannot approach the Tao
any more than separate yourself from It;
you cannot bring It favor
any more than prejudice:
you can not bestow It with honor
any more than with dishonor.
That is why It is in such high esteem all over the world.

*Lao-tzu, Tao Te Ching*[1]

\* \* \*
\* \*
\*

# THE FOUNDATIONS OF TAOISM

## LAO-TZU

Lao-tzu was born in China, some twenty years before the Buddha. His teaching shows some similarities with that of Buddhism, and the two doctrines, by mutual borrowing, with time will reach some kind of unity at the ritual and symbolic level.

The starting points of each of the two Great Sages was different. Lao-tzu comtemplated the natural harmony of the universe, whereas the Buddha considered, first of all, the inherent suffering in existence. But for both, reality issues from emptiness, the Tao. Phenomena are illusory, and the way avoids extremes and rejects dualism. To the Buddhist Hindrances, Taoism opposes a vision of the universe that transforms itself endlessly; all is mutation, and all is manifestation of the One that embraces opposites in its transcendent unity. Illumination is fusion in the Tao.

Lao-tzu's life is not well known. It is presented as a traditional legendary account rather than a factual report. Some people even maintain that Lao-tzu was a mythical person.

While he was chief of the imperial archives, Lao-tzu witnessed the downfall of the Chou Dynasty. The progressive disintegration of the spiritual forces seemed unstoppable, so the Sage decided to retire from the world and to unite with the Divine Tao. During a long journey by ox, Lao-tzu traveled through the changing landscapes of China; he created two monasteries and continued on his way, illuminated. As he was getting ready to cross the Great Wall in order to leave his country forever, the guard at the gate saw in him a great wise man and begged him not to deprive men of his teachings. Then, in a single night, Lao-tzu wrote his work, *The Tao Te Ching*. Here, in a series of vivid, mysterious and sometimes unclear sentences, he left the legacy of his teaching. Lao-tzu is one of the rare initiators of religious thought who has written his teachings himself. This is, perhaps, one of the reasons for their perfection and conciseness.

Such are the only facts that are available on the 'Old Master,' the 'Sovereign of the Obscure.' Once he had crossed the Great Wall of China, he disappeared forever, and no one knows the place and the date of his death. Tradition claims that he went to lead an ascetic life of snowy solitude in perfect unity with the Tao.

## CREATION BORN FROM NOTHINGNESS

In his work, Lao-tzu divided the Tao into two distinct levels. He wished to clarify to what degree the Tao was ungraspable and to what degree all definition and all research could lead one in the wrong direction.

The first level is that of the Absolute Tao, which escapes all definition and does not admit any conception that the mind can form.

'A way that can be laid out is not the Eternal Way, a name that can be pronounced is not the Eternal Name.'[2]

The second level is that of the Relative Tao, such as it is obscured by all definition and description. All the accounts, even those of the masters, belong to that level.

The transformation of emptiness, from the Tao to creation, passes through these two levels, the nameless and the formulated. It is from the Tao that the universe originated, and it is through forming a unity with this primary matrix that man can realize in himself universal harmony and reach deliverance:

In the beginning there was nothingness and nothingness had no name. From there was produced the One, the one without any material form. Beings were born from it: this is known as its virtue. In what had no shape, there occurred a distribution, from which followed a perpetual movement, which is called destiny. During these transformations, beings were born. At his full development, the created being possesses an organized body. This body preserves the soul. The soul and the body are submitted to their own laws. That is what is known as innate nature. Who perfects his nature returns to his original virtue. Who reaches his virtue, identifies himself with the origin of the universe, and by that, with emptiness. Emptiness is greatness. It is like the bird that sings spontaneously and identifies itself with the universe. It is when he identifies himself perfectly with the universe that he appears ignorant and obscure. He attains profound virtue and sinks into the harmony of the universe.[3]

THE CHANGES OF THE UNIVERSE

The *I Ching*, the Book of Changes, is one of the oldest Chinese treatises. It is also the one that had the most profound influence on the development of Chinese thought and philosophy. The understanding of the fusion of individual consciousness in the flux of changes has always been, for Chinese people, and long before Lao-tzu, the most satisfactory image for defining supreme wisdom – Illumination. For all the Great Sages of China, meditation on the *I Ching* was the seed of profound thought. 'The sovereign saint Yen Hsiang was standing in the middle of the circle around which everything was in a process of completion. He forgot the end and the beginning, the moment and duration. He was participating in the daily transformation of things, being only one with what cannot be changed.'

What cannot be changed is the universal matrix, the Tao Itself from which all has sprung. The Tao escapes the law of opposites, duration and change: it is emptiness itself.

What separates the common man from the wise man is that the former is not aware of the endless changes either in himself or in the universe. He does not see the perpetual renewal of matter and mind that from moment to moment, atom to atom causes everything not to remain as it was, even during the space of a second. It is in this sense that the Chinese proverb says: 'You will never descend twice into the same river.' The ordinary man is sensitive only to gross changes; those, for example, that cause the passage from life to death. Because of this, he gives great importance to death, which is composed of the tiny changes that intervene from the moment of birth. Lieh-tzu unveils this process of becoming:

The cycle of becoming never ceases. Who can understand the hidden changes of the sky and the earth? For, when things diminish on one side, they increase on the other. Here, they take full shape; there, they empty themselves. There are growth and decay that blossom and die perpetually. Their appearance and development are tied to invisible transitions. Who is attentive to it?

Nowhere can one see the force increasing all at once, or form suddenly ceasing to exist. That is why no one perceives either their expansion or their vanishing. In this way, man, from birth to old age, changes every day in his external aspect and in his aptitudes: Skin, nails and hair continuously grow and fall. No state ever stops changing. But the transitions are imperceptible. It is only after they occur that one recognizes them.[4]

### FORM AND THE LOSS OF THE TAO

Form is the result of the loss of the Tao, and vice versa. As soon as form is born, the Tao is lost. Birth is the loss of the emptiness of the Tao, and man then creates other forms that are only rough and false images of the original purity. He calls them wisdom, humanity, virtue, love, morality, and the search for these images turns him away from the Tao. Man loses himself on the road of action from which he expects well-defined fruit, and his consciousness is engulfed slowly in the illusion of purity. The will to return to the Tao is itself considered a form of darkness. 'The Tao that one tries to seize is not the true Tao,' says Lao-tzu.

This conception of the sinking of consciousness is very powerful for all wise Taoists; the more one tries, the more he loses himself in illusory forms:

All discussion implies partial vision. The supreme Tao has no name; the supreme speech does not speak; the supreme kindness excludes all partial favors; the supreme purity is without ostentation; the supreme courage is without cruelty.

The Tao explained is no longer the Tao; discursive reasoning does not reach the truth; kindness that insists is incomplete; exclusive purity does not conquer the heart; courage accompanied by cruelty does not reach its goal. All are like a circle that strives to become square.

To know that there are things that one cannot know is the summit of knowledge. The one who knows that speech is wordless and that the Tao is without name possesses the treasures of Heaven. Pouring without ever filling, imbibing without ever satisfying, and not even knowing why, this is what is called hiding the Light.[5]

## THE RETURN TO THE TAO

If wise Taoists took the trouble to leave their disciples a written doctrine, it was obviously to point out the way that leads to deliverance, to unity with the divine Tao. For the man who wishes to identify with the Tao, the way is extremely delicate, and Lieh-tzu defines clearly the necessary means:

'The Tao is not far enough away for one to have to undergo a rigorous research in order to find It; but is not close enough to be found at random.'[6]

The entire Taoist action is a progressive slipping into the silence of mind and into non-action. It is a question, for the disciple, not of gain, or of becoming rich, but of gradually getting away from any mental accumulation so that the Light may spring from emptiness. The sage forgets, he empties himself.

'By devoting oneself to study, one enlarges each day; by consecrating oneself to the Tao, one diminishes each day; one continues to diminish until reaching non-action. By non-action, there is truly nothing that cannot be done!'[7]

Two short tales of Chuang-tzu marvelously explain the way of the wise:

The Yellow Sovereign was walking to the north of the river that was the color of fire. He went up the mountain K'un-l'un, and as he was getting ready to return to the south, he noticed that he had lost *Dark Pearl*. He had Intelligence look for her but to no avail; then he sent Discernment, who also did not find her; and finally, Analysis, who did not find her either. In the end it was Without Image who found her. The Yellow Sovereign said to himself: Isn't it strange that it was Without Image who was able to find her?

The Sovereign of the South Sea was called Rapidly; the Sovereign of the North Sea was called Suddenly; the Sovereign of the Center was called Indistinction. One day, Rapidly and Suddenly met in the country of Indistinction, who treated them with much kindness. Rapidly and Suddenly wanted to reward his gracious welcome, and they said to each other: Man has seven orifices to see, listen, breathe and eat. Indistinction has none. We are going to pierce some openings for him. Setting to work, they made one opening a day for him. The seventh day, Indistinction died.[8]

Tradition teaches that Confucius himself had not yet penetrated the Tao at the age of fifty-one. He went then to his Master, Lao Tan (Lao-tzu), who asked him what had been his way. Confucius recalled the five years he spent studying mathematics, the twelve years studying the darkness and the light and said that, besides, he knew Six Books perfectly: The Odes, History, Poetry, Music, The Changes, and last of all, the book of the two Springs and Autumn. Lao Tan then told him about the Tao, and Confucius retired to a hut for three months. He came back to his master and said to him:

'I have understood now. The crows and the magpies incubate their eggs, and fish plan their spawning; the locust engenders itself by metamorphosis; the birth of the younger brother makes the older cry. For a long time now I haven't participated in these transformations. He who does not participate in transformation, how could he transform other men?'

'That is right, says Lao Tan, you have felt the Tao.'[9]

## SIMPLE LIFE, SPONTANEITY, NON-ACTION

The simple life, spontaneity and non-action are the main qualities of the Taoist adept as he learns about the Tao. He often renounces the world and goes to a peaceful hermitage where he contemplates life, whose changes appear to him with greater and greater sharpness. Non-action does not mean that the ascetic does nothing; it only means that there is no tie between himself and action, and there is no desire, no ownership, no expectation of any

result. The act is born in necessity and falls again into forgetfulness. It is an absolutely pure and spontaneous spouting that is the
manifestation of emptiness. Every action is in agreement with the
Tao, and fullness is attained.

Searching for the Tao means, first of all, eliminating everything
that is not indispensable to physical life. Then, in the contemplation of nature, Illumination occurs. All manifestation becomes
manifestation of the Tao.

Chinese poetry has been very strongly influenced by Taoism,
and many poems sing the simple joys of the person who is alone:

### Looking for Master Yung Ts'un in His Hermitage

Among the peaks whose emerald touches the sky,
You live freely, forgetting the years.
I part the clouds to search for the old road:
I dwell on the grass to listen to the springs.

In the warmth of flowers, the black oxen lie;
On the high pines, the white cranes are sleeping.
While we are speaking, the twilight is falling on the river;
And alone, I go down in the cold and the mist.[10]
*Li Po*

*For President Sine from my Lonely Hermitage in the Mountain*

Between mountains and valleys, a clear landscape is purified;
And the clarity of the landscape sculptures the mountains and the valleys.
The flight of the white clouds colors at dawn;
The cloud of the green waters raises its clear voice.

In front of the door, the gorge spreads a residue of color;
Under the window, the mountain thickens the shade of night.
The grasses and the flowers assemble their contrasts;
The trees and the rocks assault the heights.

Sitting all alone in front of the woven pallet;
I have no visitor, but I have my singing lute.
In the silence and the peace of the mountains,
Who can know the peace of my heart?
*Yang Sou*

*He Who Is Alone*

See the trees that grow on the knoll:
Each has its own heart.
See the birds that sing in the woods:
Each has its own melody.
See the fish that swim in the river:
One floats, another dives.
The height of the mountains is dizzying,
The depth of the waters unfathomable!
The appearance of things is easy to see,
But their principle comes from an arduous quest;
*Emperor Non of Liang*[11]

He who is alone no longer allows his mental powers to comment on daily events. Sensations pass, fleeting and without any other connection than the one they have with the Tao, which engulfs everything. He who is alone slides into the heart of each movement, of each trembling, and appearances no longer have any hold over him. The untrodden zone of the entire psychological past extends day by day and he who is alone enjoys a freedom that is more and more complete. He empties himself, he purifies himself and unites himself with the Tao. He reflects change, without monopolizing it, and he gives the instrument of his body to the harmony of the universe.

This return by means of physical and mental silence to original purity restores to the senses a sharpness that the repeated assault of the emotions had made them lose. In Taoism, this return to the primordial state is very important, and it is situated at all levels of being. The journey of him who is alone is the total return to the primordial state:

The five colors blind the sight of man,
The five sounds deafen the hearing of man,
The five flavors spoil the taste of man,
The struggles and trials misguide the heart of the man.
The search for treasures excites man to commit evil.

That is why the holy man looks after his belly and not his eye.
That is why he rejects this and chooses that.[12]

He who refines his vision puts disorder into the five colors and introduces deformity into lines and drawings. He dazzles people by his greens, his yellows, and by the brightness of his embellishments. . . .

He who refines hearing puts disorder into the five tones and introduces dissonance into the six musical pipes. He overwhelms people by the noise of metal, stone, silk, the bamboo of Huang-ch'ung and Ta-lei . .[13]

Finally, Non-Action is clarified by this anecdote of Chuang-tzu, who shows how the sage accomplishes what has to be, without the anticipation of thought, without control of thought, and without analyzing the why and the how of the spontaneous act:

Confucius admired the cataracts of Lin-liang, which measured thirty fathoms and whose foam spread over 800 yards. In this foam, neither giant turtle, nor soft-shell turtle, nor alligator, nor fish could gambol. Suddenly, Confucius saw an old man swimming in the eddies. Taking him for a madman, he gave the order to his disciple to follow the bank and pull him out of the water. A few hundred steps below, the man got out of the water by himself. Hair dishevelled, singing, he walked down the slope. When Confucius met up with him, he said to him: 'I almost took you for a spirit, but I see that you are a man. Allow me to ask what your method is that enables you to swim so easily in the water.'

'I have no particular method. I began by habit; then it became natural; then it became my destiny. I go down with the whirlpools and come back up with the eddies. I obey the movement of the water, not my own will. That is how I manage to swim in the water so easily.'

'What do you mean by: I began by habit; I perfected myself naturally; it has become as natural as my destiny?'

'I was born in these hills and I have lived with ease; that is habit; I grew up in the water and I find myself at ease there; that is nature; thus I swim without knowing how, that is destiny.'[14]

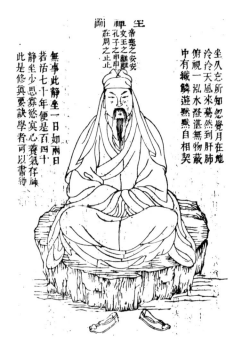

The Tao is like a vase
that use never fills.
It is like a gulf,
the origin of everything in the world.

It takes the edge off every blade,
It unties all skeins,
It blends all lights,
It unites all particles.

It seems very profound,
It seems to last forever.
Son of I don't know whom
it has to be the ancestor of the Gods.

*Lao-tzu, Tao Te Ching*[1]

\* \* \*
\* \*
\*

## CHAPTER NINE

# TAOIST CONTEMPLATIVE TECHNIQUES

## FORGETTING WHAT ONE KNOWS

Forgetfulness is the most important way to the gate of contemplation. It is necessary to empty oneself of all forms that constitute the external man so that the liberated spirit may receive the Light. The Light requires a mental vacuum in order to illuminate the totality of being. The Master's task is to guide his disciple toward this laying bare. Forgetting what is so deeply anchored in us is one of the hardest things to do:

During the time Lieh-tzu was a disciple, he took three years to unlearn the habit of judging and of qualifying with words. Then, his master Lao-Shang honored him with a look for the first time.

After five years, he neither judged nor qualified, even in thought. Then his master Lao-Shang smiled at him for the first time.

At the end of seven years, when even the distinction between yes and no, between advantage and disadvantage had been wiped from his mind, his master allowed him to sit on his mat for the first time.

At the end of nine years, after he had lost the notion of just and unjust, and of good and evil, relative to self and to others, when he had become absolutely indifferent to everything, the perfect communion between the external world and his profound depths was established in him. He stopped using his senses. His mind solidified to such a degree that his body dissolved, his flesh and bones liquified. He lost all sensation of the mat on which he was sitting, of the ground that supported his feet. He lost the understanding of formulated ideas, and of spoken words. Thus, he reached that state where nothing in the natural order was obscure for him any more.[2]

The more forgetfulness attains the depths of being, the more the original mind, which by itself participates in Tao, is revealed. Its nature is pure, calm and without image. The conscious mind that participates in the game of the intellect is troubled and agitated. It continuously obscures the original mind by its endless activity. It lives off the energy of purity, and progressively gains control of its substance until it is completely exhausted. Everything in the Taoists' contemplative practices is a game of opposite energies. Each external form possesses its profound form and thus creates a subtle double of the individual such as he appears to us.


### THE PREPARATION FOR MEDITATION


*The meditation room* is the secret place where the body and mind must establish themselves in tranquillity. Many conditions have to be met. Here is one of the meticulous descriptions from a Taoist manuscript of the ninth or tenth century, quoted by Henri Maspero:

That is why, when one wishes to devote himself to this exercise, it is necessary to take a separate room, well whitewashed with a fragrant coating of good clay, with a proper light, high and wide, with a bed with a thick warm mattress with freshly washed blankets and pillow. No one who is impure must be allowed inside. The floor inside should be dug to a depth of two feet, and sifted to get rid of mud and gravel; it is necessary to remove anything that is unclean. Then, with a coating of good clay, build a platform of packed clay; then again pack the soil with finely sifted clay so that it is very firm. . . . In the room, place only a writing table and a coffer to hold the books of *Ching-kuei*. Every time you enter, light the incense and meditate on the Venerable Celestial–Mysterious–Original– without–Superior Hsüan-yuan Wu-shang T'ien-ts'un; and again, meditate on the True Lord the Great One T'ai-i Chen- chün.[3]

*The position of meditation* can be the lotus position previously described, or the prostrate position adopted by Taoist monks.

When one of these positions is adopted, it is recommended to focus on the end of the nose, or on a point on the ground in a straight line with the nose. On one hand, this avoids distractions caused by fixing the look straight ahead. It also prevents the mind from wandering into dreams and the drowsiness induced by closed eyes. It is next necessary to fix the mind on the yellow center, the point situated between the eyebrows, to allow the light to spread inside the body and purify it. The mind is thus crysallized on one spot, which facilitates the arrival of deep concentration.

Lu Tzu, in *The Secret of the Golden Flower*, summarizes the state of the meditator as follows:

The eye is not looking upward, the eyelids are lowered, and it shines towards what is inward. It shines on this spot. The mouth does not speak or laugh. One shuts the lips and breathes inwardly. Breathing is here. The nose does not smell odors. Smell is here. The ear does not hear external things. Hearing is here. The entire heart watches what is inward. Its watching is here. The thoughts do not flow outwardly. True thoughts possess time by themselves. If the thoughts are lasting, the seed is lasting; if the seed is lasting the energy is lasting; if the energy is lasting, the mind is lasting. Mind is thought, thought is heart, heart is fire, fire is the golden bud. When one contemplates inwardly in this way, the wonders of the opening and closing of the doors of heaven become inexhaustible. But if one does not breathe rhythmically, one cannot realize the most profound mysteries.[4]

In order to adopt the prostrate position, the Taoist meditator lies on his bed, on his side, with legs folded in, the body raised by a round cushion placed under the armpit and on which the arm leans to hold up the head. The other arm rests on the thigh, and the hand on the knee. This posture, besides being very comfortable, is peculiar to China where it has many followers, although the treatises more often utilize the classical lotus position.

*The hours favorable for meditation* are related to the inspirations and expirations of the universe, which is comparable to a human body. The day is divided into two parts; the first, the night, which is Yin (feminine), and the second, the day, which is Yang (masculine). The time of inspiration corresponds to Yang, the day, and the time of expiration to Yin, the night.

The two most beneficial moments for contemplation are at the time of the inspiration of new energies, namely, at the moment when the night air begins to warm up, just before sunrise, and in the evening, at the moment of sunset, when the air of day begins to cool off by contact with the night.

Taoists do not stop at this division of time, and have determined the hours of day in which the energies are Yin and those in which the energies are Yang:

From 3 am to 5 am, Yang.
From 5 am to 7 am, Yin.
From 7 am to 9 am, Yang.
From 9 am to 11 am, Yin.
From 11 am to 1 pm, Yang.
From 1 pm to 3 pm, Yin.
From 3 pm to 5 pm, Yang.

From 5 pm to 7 pm, Yin.
From 7 pm to 9 pm, Yang.
From 9 pm to 11 pm, Yin.
From 11 pm to 1 am, Yang.
From 1 am to 3 am, Yin.

## IMMORTALITY AND THE TAOIST BODY

Taoists conceive eternal life as the immortality of the subtle body
of man, which is liberated from its gross envelope after death. This
subtle body is a progressive material transmutation that inter-
venes due to contemplative practices, but also due to alimentary
diets that balance the energies of Yin and Yang, as well as to
alchemy, to medicine and to the art of keeping and of transmuting
the seed during sexual union.

During this passage of one body to the other, the contents are
transformed: the flesh becomes jade and the bones, gold.

It is breathing that propels the blood in the body and makes it
circulate. Each inhalation and each exhalation make it advance
three inches inside the veins and arteries. A human has an average
of 13,500 respiratory movements a day, so the blood circulates a
total distance of 81,000 feet a day. In one day, the blood makes 50
complete revolutions in the body.

A perfectly regulated and rythmical breathing thus provides a
progressive and equal irrigation of the entire body, and puts it in a
position of perfect equilibrium that renders it capable of receiving
the Light.

The body itself is divided into three sections. The upper section
is from the head to the base of the neck. The middle section is
from the base of the neck to the diaphragm, and the lower section
is from the diaphragm to the sexual organs. The diaphragm marks
the separation between the upper Yang half and the Yin half
below. Each of the three sections possesses a field of Vermilion, or
main part.

The divinities (there are 36,000) reside inside the body, which
is the image of the cosmos. Each of them resides in a precise point
of the body where its celestial palaces and its followers are found.
A supreme god, the Great One, gathers and unifies the many energies of the 36,000 gods. The existence of these gods inside the
body is made possible by the real size of the body, which is that of

the universe as it was represented in the past: the earth and the celestial arch. The sun and the moon are the left eye and the right eye, the veins are small rivers and the arteries are large rivers; head hair and body hair are the stars and the planets. They are where the gods have their palaces. The gods amuse themselves but take no active part in the life of the universe. The ceaseless mutations unfold without the interference of anyone. Everyone knows that a divine intervention in the progress of the evolution of the world would occur as a catastrophe.

In order for the gross body to be transformed into the subtle body after death, it is necessary for the gods to remain inside the body. For this, a man must have known them during his life, frequented them, and localized them in himself. He should also have walked each day in the innumerable palaces where the divinities are rejoicing. This is the object of meditation.

## THE INTERIOR VISION

Settle in a calm and secluded place, sitting or lying, close the eyes to blot out external vision, and after a few exercises, you will begin to see the inside of the body, the fine visceras, the twelve veins and all the organs, as well as the blood that circulates and the breath that travels through them. Turn the eyes that are the sun and the moon inward and illuminate the darkness. If that doesn't work, there are formulas to make the sun and the moon come down from the sky, and make them enter the body in order to illuminate it.[5]

The mind must be pure and the heart empty if contact with the powers is to be established. If the meditator tries to enter into communication with the spirits of his body when his inner state is contaminated or agitated, the ill-omened divinities will appear and take possession of him.

This knowledge of the gods inside one's own cosmic body is progressive. When one has emptied the mind of all agitation, one begins by entering in contact with the lesser powers, and it is they who guide the adept towards deeper ecstasies, during which he will encounter more and more powerful divinities. All these divinities have habits with which the adept must first become familiar. He learns to recognize their physical aspect, he sees their ornaments and their attributes in detail, and then he knows where they prefer to dwell. He also learns to approach them, to speak to them and to assess the well-defined powers of each one of them. Then, little by little, the powers will come and help him, and for every situation, he will know whom to ask for assistance. Little by little, the adept will cross all the barriers, and when he knows the supreme divinities, his mind will be illuminated and he will be identified with the Divine Tao, in a final ecstasy. Illumination, however, is not progressive. It is sudden. Only the preparation of following the middle road, which avoids an excessive search as well as a premature complete abandonment, will one day allow the blossoming of the Tao.

Illumination resembles a leap over a gulf or an abyss. Either one leaps over the abyss, or else one remains the way he was.[6]

Thirty spokes converge to the hub,
but it is the middle emptiness that
makes the chariot go.

One works clay in order to make vases,
but it is the internal emptiness
on which their usage depends.

A house is cut with doors and windows,
again, it is emptiness
that permits the dwelling.

Being gives possibilities,
it is through non-being that one uses them.[7]

### THE ART OF HARMONIZING THE BREATH

All Taoist treatises insist heavily on the practice of rhythmical breathing. Without its mastery, the states of superior ecstasy cannot be reached.

The universe itself is created by the differentiation of breaths that brought form from chaos. Nine distinct breaths sprang from chaos and gave birth to the powers. Light and darkness separated and the cosmos was formed from a coagulation of nine breaths; the unused residues of this creative breath are those that are still circulating in the world under the name of internal breath. It is these that the Taoists absorb in order to obtain immortality. This breath, obviously, is not the one that we absorb by breathing (external breath), but it is the creative power that resides inside ourselves. The most ancient Taoist theories maintain, however, that the absorbtion of the external breath renders the body immortal.

## RETENTION AND CIRCULATION OF THE EXTERNAL BREATH

The first Taoists substituted the pure nourishment of the breath for coarse nourishment by slowly absorbing the external air, and by keeping it as long as possible in the body. This allowed the absorption of the energy with which it was loaded. It then was released through the mouth.

Settle in a secluded room, lock the doors, sit on a soft-matted pallet with a pillow 2½ inches high. Lie down with the body in the correct position, close the eyes and hold the breath locked in the diaphragm of the chest to such a degree that a hair placed on the nose and mouth does not move.[8]

## THE GREAT CIRCULATION OF BREATH THROUGH THE BODY

All these exercises have to be accompanied by an intense concentration that follows the breath as it becomes a warm stream in its journey inside the body. Every atom of the body is thus touched by the breath.

The great circulation of the breath through the body is divided into two stages. The ascendant circulation, which goes from the coccyx to the top of the head, is called *t'o mu*, or *controlled course*. The descendant circulation, which goes from the head to rejoin the coccyx, passing by the chest and the stomach, is called *jen mu* or *involuntary course*.

Taoist respiratory technique recommends at the outset a profound, slow, rhythmical inhalation and exhalation. The absorbed air must be sent as far as the abdomen; it is for this reason that the center of the loins, below the navel, is called the Sea of Breath. When one exhales, the diaphragm raises and the abdomen becomes hollow, which is the opposite of what happens when one inhales.[9]

What crosses and bathes the body is not the breath itself, but the energy of the breath that the meditator directs through concentration to any part of his body, when his training is adequate.

The mastery of breathing goes along with the development of the Light. For that, breathing must be subtle:

While one is sitting, he has to keep his heart peaceful and his energy gathered. How can one render the heart peaceful? By means of breathing. The heart alone must be conscious of the ebb and flow of breathing. It should not be heard by the ears. If breathing cannot be heard, it is because it is subtle; if it is subtle, then it is pure. If the breathing can be heard, it means the energy of the breathing is coarse; if it is coarse, then it is dull; if it is dull, then indolence and torpor appear and one wants to sleep.[10]

Therefore, by concentrating on the yellow center, the point situated between the eyebrows, the Light will be born. The meditator will experience a deep joy, and a great luminous power will invade him. He will be bathed in it, and the Light will be so powerful that it will gush forth and spread out into the space. It is what Lu Tzu calls the formation of the Bud of the Golden Flower, the beginning of contemplation. Next, all perception ceases; the meditator will unite with the Divine Tao.

One of the original things about the Taoist way is that it does not advise the meditators to retire from the world, although that becomes, eventually, the ideal of the Sage.

When one arrives progressively at evoking the revolution of the light, it is not necessary to renounce one's habitual preoccupations. The ancients said:

When affairs come to us, accept them; when things come to us, it is necessary to explore them deeply. When one puts his affairs in order by means of correct thought, the Light is not dictated by external things, but the Light turns according to its own law. In this way, even the still invisible revolution of the Light can be released and even more importantly, the true and pure revolution of the Light that has already made its clear appearance.

When in ordinary life one is constantly able to react to things by reflex without mixing any thoughts concerning oneself or others, it is a revolution of the Light born from circumstances. This is the principal secret.[11]

## THE ABSORPTION AND THE UTILIZATION
## OF THE INTERNAL BREATH

Man, in being born, receives the Original Breath from Heaven and from Earth, which becomes his spirit and his body, and he receives the breath from the Original One, which becomes his saliva and his essence.[12]

Therefore, one must not let this breath escape, which is that of life itself. Then, the Field of Vermilion situated under the navel will be filled by it. One should keep this subtle breath from leaving the body by mingling with external breathing.

The internal breath occurs naturally in the body, and it is not a breath that one searches for externally. But if one does not obtain the correct explanations from an enlightened master, all attempts will end in useless fatigue and never succeed.[13]

The internal breath follows the same circuit as the external one. There are two ways to make it circulate inside the body.

1. The adept controls the breath by his own concentration and directs it toward the organs that he needs to reach in order to stimulate or heal them.
2. The adept follows the natural way by letting the breath go by itself to the organs that need it. He thus follows this path without letting his will intervene.

The method for swallowing breath is as follows:

Both the nose and the mouth are shut and completely empty, so that the internal breath fills the mouth; beat the celestial drum fifteen times, or more – the more the better; as if you were swallowing a large gulp of water, make the internal breath in the mouth enter the belly; through concentration, lead it to the Field of Vermilion.[14]

There are two methods for directing this breath:

Some are content to visually represent the breath while it makes its journey through the body. Others use a process common with Taoists. In this process, the imagination creates a dwarf charged with the direction of the breath and followed by thought all through the voyage. . . . Thus, one directs the breath through the body, as slowly and as completely as possible.[15]

## THE ART OF YIN AND YANG THAT PROLONGS LIFE

Aside from the techniques of alchemy, which do not concern us here, the Taoists had great esteem for what they called the art of Yin and Yang that prolongs life. That is to say, the art of balancing the two vital principles and of charging the body with physical energy by practicing sexual union and conserving the semen.

At the moment of orgasm, when it is not released, but brought back by the force of thought, it penetrates into the crucible of the creator, and refreshes and nourishes the heart and the body. This is called the method of reversal. For this reason, it is said: The Way of the Golden Bud rests completely on the method of reversal.[16]

If one begins to apply this magical method, it is as if, at the center of being, there was non-being. Thus, in time, when the work is finished and it happens that there is a body beyond the body, it is then only that it becomes spiritual fire. After a hundred days, in the center of the Light one will see a point of the true luminous pole appearing from him. Then, suddenly, the germinal pearl appears. It is similar to the conception that takes place when a man and a woman unite. Thus, one can remain perfectly calm while waiting for it. The revolution of the Light is the era of fire.[17]

Essence, or sperm, is thus a precious material not only for the ascetic who transforms it into psychic energy, but also for the ordinary man, who considerably diminishes his mental and physical power by wasting it. These conceptions are prevalent, and all the great mystical traditions have applied their principles. Still, the Taoists claim that the conservation of essence is not enough. It is necessary to increase its power by uniting it with the feminine Yin, and by mastering the body with the mind, or by using the technique of retention that will be explained later.

However, chastity is not recommended, because the Taoists do not find it very natural. It is necessary to unite instead, with as many women as possible, without losing essence:

The Jade Emperor lay with 1,200 women and became immortal; the common people have only one woman and destroy their life.[18]

As an ideal partner, the treatises recommend taking a young girl between fourteen and nineteen years old, who knows nothing of these procedures. She should be childless, her breasts should not be too developed, and she should have a healthy body. Her hair and body hair must be fine. Her voice should be sweet and harmonious and her bones invisible under flesh whose skin is soft.

But what is important is to avoid those with certain defects, of which there is a long list: those who have thick skin, those who are too skinny, those who have a masculine voice and breathe heavily, those who have hair on the legs, those who are jealous, those whose sexual parts are cold, those who eat too much, those who are more than 40 years old, those who always have a cold body, those who have strong and hard bones, those who have an uncouth smell, etc.[19]

The greater the number of partners in the same night, the greater the benefit. The ritual can also be performed collectively, but certain conditions have to be observed. It should be done on the day of the full moon or the new moon, after three days of fasting and meditation. Choose a clear, calm, limpid night. Be perfectly calm and without any violent emotions. Be in possession of all your physical and psychic force, and have no fear or apprehension. Do not take drugs or alcohol. Finally, the temperature should be neither too hot nor too cold, and the air should be pleasantly perfumed. If one adheres to all the precepts, then there are more than two hundred days a year when the sexual union is ill-omened for those who practise it.

Forget the world, lose consciousness of the external phenomena, enter into a profound concentration, eliminate all thought and control breathing. It is also necessary to focus the mind on the loins in order to follow the ascendency of the energy.

Slow foreplay is important each time one lies with a woman so that the spirits will be in harmony. It is only when the spirits are perfectly moved for a long time that the couple can unite.

Go in when the penis is soft and pull it back out when it becomes firm and strong. Penetrate only without ejaculating. He who can have intercourse many times in a single day and a single night without letting his essence escape will be healed of all disease, and his longevity will increase. Changing women several times is more advantageous; if one has ten different women in one night, there will be a supreme degree of excellence.[20]

The essential of Taoist sexual practices consists not only in being able to preserve the essence, but, above all, to make it rise so as to illuminate the psyche:

The principle of making the essence return in order to heal the brain consists in copulating in order to render the essence very agitated; then, when it is about to come out, one quickly seizes the penis with the two middle fingers of the left hand behind the scrotum and in front of the anus, pressing firmly, and expelling a long breath through the mouth, while grinding the teeth a great number of times without retaining the breath. Then, when one emits the essence, it cannot get out, but returns to the Jade Stem (the penis) and mounts to the brain.[21]

The adept then experiences ecstasy and light. He is flooded with beneficial strength and his power increases considerably.

When a superior spirit hears the Tao,
he practices it with zeal.
When an average spirit hears the Tao,

sometimes he keeps it, sometimes he loses it.
When an inferior spirit hears the Tao,
he roars with laughter;
if he did not laugh at it
the Tao would no longer be the Tao.

   For the Adage says:

The road of the Light looks dark.
The road of progress seems backwards.
The even road seems uneven.
The supreme virtue seems empty.
The supreme candor seems soiled.
The superabundant virtue seems insufficient.
The solid virtue seems negligent.
The profound virtue seems fluctuating.
The great square has no angles.
The great vase is slow to perfect.
The great music hardly has sounds.
The great image has no form.
The hidden Tao has no name.
And yet, it alone
sustains and completes all beings.[22]

## *The Supreme Void*

Attain the supreme void
and remain in silence.
In front of the teeming agitation of beings,
contemplate only the return.

The many beings of the world
will return to their roots.
To return to the road is to be installed in silence.
To be installed in silence is to find order again.
To find order again is to know constancy.
To know constancy is Illumination.

Who does not know constancy
blindly creates his unhappiness.
Who knows constancy will be tolerant.
Who is tolerant will be disinterested.
Who is disinterested will be royal.
Who is royal will be celestial.
Who is celestial will be one with the Tao.

Who is one with the Tao will live a long time.
Until the end of his life, nothing will be able to touch him.[23]

## The Empty Infinity

Without beginning, without end
without past, without future.
One halo of light surrounds the world of the mind.
Mutually one forgets the other, calm and pure,
full of power and emptiness.
The water of the sea is smooth and reflects
light on its surface.
The clouds disappear in azure space.
The mountains shine transparently.
Consciousness dissolves in contemplation.
The disk of the moon remains in solitude.[24]

掃石焚香任意眠醒來時有客談玄

松風不用蒲葵扇坐對滿崖百丈泉

古洞幽深絕世人石床風細不生塵

日長一覺羲皇睡又見峯頭上月輪

卧

開心宗之性

示不動之體

悟夢覺之真

人間思之寂

禪

人間白月醒猶睡老子·山中睡却醒

醒睡兩非逺兩是溪雲漠漠水泠泠

闢

元神夜夜宿丹田雲滿黃庭月滿天

兩簡篤篤浮綠水水心一朵紫金蓮

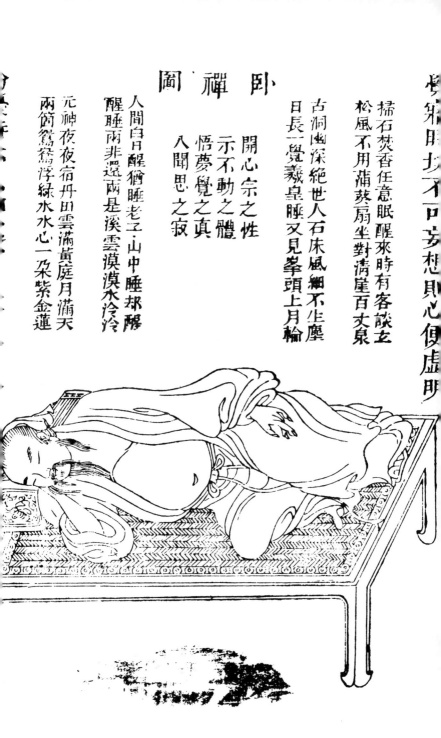

*Map*                    183

## THE SPREAD OF BUDDHISM

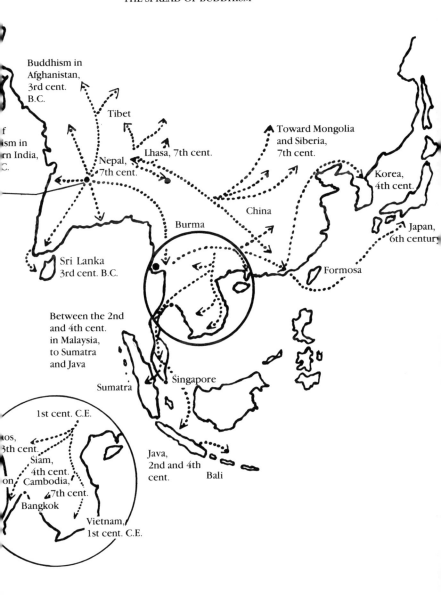

Buddhism in
Afghanistan,
3rd cent.
B.C.

Tibet

f
ism in
rn India,
C.

Lhasa, 7th cent.

Nepal,
7th cent.

Toward Mongolia
and Siberia,
7th cent.

Korea,
4th cent.

China

Japan,
6th century

Burma

Formosa

Sri Lanka
3rd cent. B.C.

Between the 2nd
and 4th cent.
in Malaysia,
to Sumatra
and Java

Singapore

Sumatra

1st cent. C.E.

os,
th cent.

Siam,
4th cent.

Java,
2nd and 4th
cent.

Bali

on  Cambodia,
7th cent.

Bangkok

Vietnam,
1st cent. C.E.

# FOOTNOTES

* * *

* *

*

## Chapter 1

1   Maurice Perchoron, *Le Bouddha*, Seuil, Paris, 1956.
2   *La Vie merveilleuse du Bouddha*, De Duca, Paris, 1956.
3   Ibid.
4   Ibid.
5   *Choix de Jâtaka*, French version translated from Pali by Ginette Terral, Gallimard, 1958.

## Chapter 2

1   Grimn, Georges, *La Religion du Bouddha*, A. Maisonneuve, Paris, 1959.
2   Ibid.
3   *Dyâna pour les débutants*, A. Maisonneuve, Paris, 1951.

## Chapter 3

1   *Satipatthana, le coeur de la méditation bouddhiste*, A. Maisonneuve, Paris.
2   *Le Chemin des nuages blancs*, Albin Michel, Paris, 1969.
3   *Mystiques et magiciens du Tibet*, Plon, Paris.
4   A. Maisonneuve, Paris, 1951.
5   A. David–Neel and Lama Yongden, *la Connaissance Transcendante*, Adyar, Paris, 1958.
6   *Livre tibetain de la grande libération*, Adyar, Paris, 1954.

## Chapter 4

1   *Satipatthana, le Coeur de la méditation bouddhiste*, A. Maisonneuve, Paris.
2   Ibid.
3   *Le Bouddhisme*, Ed. Du Rocher, Monaco, 1936.
4   Ibid.
5   A. Maisonneuve, *Satipatthana*, A. Maisonneuve, Paris.
6   A. David–Neel, *Le Bouddhisme*, Ed. du Rocher, Monaco, 1936.
7   Ibid.
8   Ibid.

## Chapter 5

1   *Milarepa*, coll. documents spirituels, Fayard, Paris, 1971.
2   E. Gonge, *le Bouddhisme dans son essence et son développement*, Payot, Paris, 1952.
3   W.Y. Evans–Wentz, Maisonneuve, A., *Le Yoga Tibétain et les doctrine secrètes*, Paris, 1964.
4   A. David–Neel, and Lama Yongden, Adyar, Paris, 1958.

## Chapter 6

1 *Tch'an (Zen), textes Chinois fondamentaux, etc*, Hermès, Paris, 1970.

## Chapter 7

1 *Les entretiens de Lin–Tsi*, Fayard, Paris, 1972.
2 *Discours et sermons de Houei–Nêng, sixième patriarche zen*, Albin Michel, Paris, 1963.
3 Op. cit.
4 Éditions traditionnelles, Paris, 1968.
5 *Anthologie de la poésie classique chinoise*, coll. Connaissance de l'Orient. Gallimard, Paris, 1969.
6 Houeï–Neng, op. cit.
7 Lin–Tsi, op. cit.
8 Op. cit.
9 Op. cit.
10 Op. cit.
11 Op. cit.
12 Marc de Smedt, *Être Jésus*, coll. Aux origines du Sacré, Laffont, Paris, 1974.
13 Hermès, op. cit.
14 Op. cit.

## Chapter 8

1 Coll. Idées, Gallimard, Paris, 1967.
2 *Tao Tö King*, published under the direction of Jean Herbert, Dervy-livres, Paris, 1969.
3 Op. cit.
4 Lie-Tseu *Le Vrai Classique du Vide Parfait*, Gallimard, Paris, 1961.
5 Tchouang–Tseu, *Oeuvres complètes*, Gallimard, Paris, 1969.
6 Lie–Tseu, op. cit.
7 Tchouang–Tseu, op. cit.
8 The Tao.
9 Tchouang–Tseu, op. cit.
10 *Anthologie de la poésie classique chinose*, Gallimard, Paris, 1969.
11 Ibid.
12 *Tao Tö King*, Gallimard, op. cit.
13 Tchouang Tseu, op. cit
14 Tchouang–Tseu, op. cit.

## Chapter 9

1 Gallimard, Paris, 1967.
2 Lie–Tseu, op. cit.
3 *Essais sur le Taoïsme*, Gallimard, Paris, 1971.
4 Librare de Médicis, Paris, 1969.
5 Henri Maspero, op. cit.
6 Chang Chung–Yuan, *Le Monde du Tao*, Stock, Paris, 1941.
7 *Tao Tö King*, op. cit.

8   Henri Maspero, op. cit.
9   *Le Monde du Tao*, op. cit.
10  Lu–Tsou, op. cit.
11  Lu–Tsou, op. cit.
12  Henri Maspero, op. cit.
13  Ibid.
14  Ibid.
15  Ibid.
16  Lu–Tsou, op. cit.
17  Lu–Tsou, op. cit.
18  Henri Maspero, op. cit.
19  Henri Maspero, op. cit.
20  Ibid.
21  Ibid.
22  Lao–Tseu, *Tao Tö King*, Gallimard, Paris, 1967.
23  Ibid.
24  Lu–Tsou, op. cit.

# S E L E C T E D   B I B L I O G R A P H Y

*   *   *
*   *
*

Benoit, Hubert. *The Supreme Doctrine*. New York: Inner Traditions International, 1984.

Benoit, Hubert. *Let Go. Theory and Practice of Detachment According to Zen*. New York: Samuel Wieser, 1973.

Blofield, John, trans. *The Zen Teaching of Huang Po*. New York: Grove Press, 1958.

Chang Chung-yuan. *Creativity and Taoism*. New York: Harper & Row, 1970.

Ch'en, Kenneth. *Buddhism In China*. Princeton: Princeton University Press, 1964.

Chuang-tzu. *Chuang-tzu: Basic Writings*. Translated by Burton Watson. New York: Columbia University Press, 1964.

Conze, Edward. *Buddhism, Its Essence and Development*. New York: Harper & Row, 1959.

Coomaraswamy, Ananda. *Hinduism and Buddhism*. New York: Philosophical Library, 1943.

Cowell, E. B. *Buddhist Mahayana Texts*. New York: Dover, 1969.

David–Neel, Alexandra. *Magic and Mystery in Tibet*. New York: Dover Publications, Inc., 1971.

Evans Wentz, W.Y., (trans.) *The Tibetan Book of the Dead*. Oxford: Oxford University Press, 1957.

Evans–Wentz, W.Y. *The Tibetan Book of the Great Liberation*. London: Oxford University Press, 1968.

Govinda, Anagarika. *Foundations of Tibetan Mysticism*. London: Rider & Co., 1960.

Hoover, Thomas. *Zen Culture*. New York: Vintage Books, 1978.

Humphreys, C. *Concentration And Meditation*. Baltimore: Penguin, 1968.

*I Ching*. Bollingen Series XIX. Princeton University Press, 1977.

Kapleau, Philip., ed. *The Three Pillars of Zen*. Boston: Beacon Press, 1967.

Lao–tzu. *The Way of Life According to Lao-tzu*. Translated by Witter Bynner. New York: G. P. Putnam's Sons, 1980.

Linssen, Robert. *Living Zen*. New York: Grove Press, 1960.

Luk, Charles. *Ch'an and Zen Teachings*. 3 Vols. London: Rider, 1962.

A.F. Price, and Wong, Mou-Lam., trans., *The Diamond Sutra and Sutra of Hui Neng*. Berkeley: Shambala, 1969.

Rahula, Walpola. *What the Buddha Taught*. New York: Grove Press, 1959.

Ramanan, Venkata. *Nargarjuna's Philosophy*. New Delhi: Motilal Banarsidass, 1975.

Rinpoche, Kalo. *Basic Writings of Kalo Rinpoche*. Translated by Ken MacLeod. Vancouver: Kagyu Kunchab Choling, 1976.

Suzuki, D. T. *Outlines of Mahayana Buddhism*. New York: Shocken, 1963.

Suzuki, D. T. *The Zen Doctrine of No Mind*. New York: Samuel Wieser, 1973.

Trungpa, Chogyam. *Meditation in Action.* Boulder: Shambhala Publications, 1969.

Tucci, Guiseppe. *Theory and Practice of Mandala.* London: Rider & Co., 1969.

Watts, A. *The Way of Zen.* New York: Vintage Books, 1957.

Watts A. *Tao the Watercourse Way.* New York: Pantheon, 1975.

# SOURCE OF ILLUSTRATIONS

\*   \*   \*
\*   \*
\*

Author's photos
Pages 5, 9, 21, 27, 35, 36, 37, 41, 47, 54, 55, 56, 57, 58, 59, 65, 74, 75, 76, 84, 93, 102, 103, 114, 115, 119, 123, 127, 129, 142, 143, 191

Photos E.R.L. (author's collection)
Pages 13, 14, 28, 42, 66, 94, 97, 120, 126

Photos E.R.L. (collection of Michel Courtois)
Page 134

Photos E.R.L. Bibliotheque Nationale
Pages 155, 159, 163

MISSI-PHOTO
Page 153

Photos Bibliotheque Nationale
Pages 156, 166, 181

*Portrait of Daniel Odier by Khempo Kalo Rinpoche*

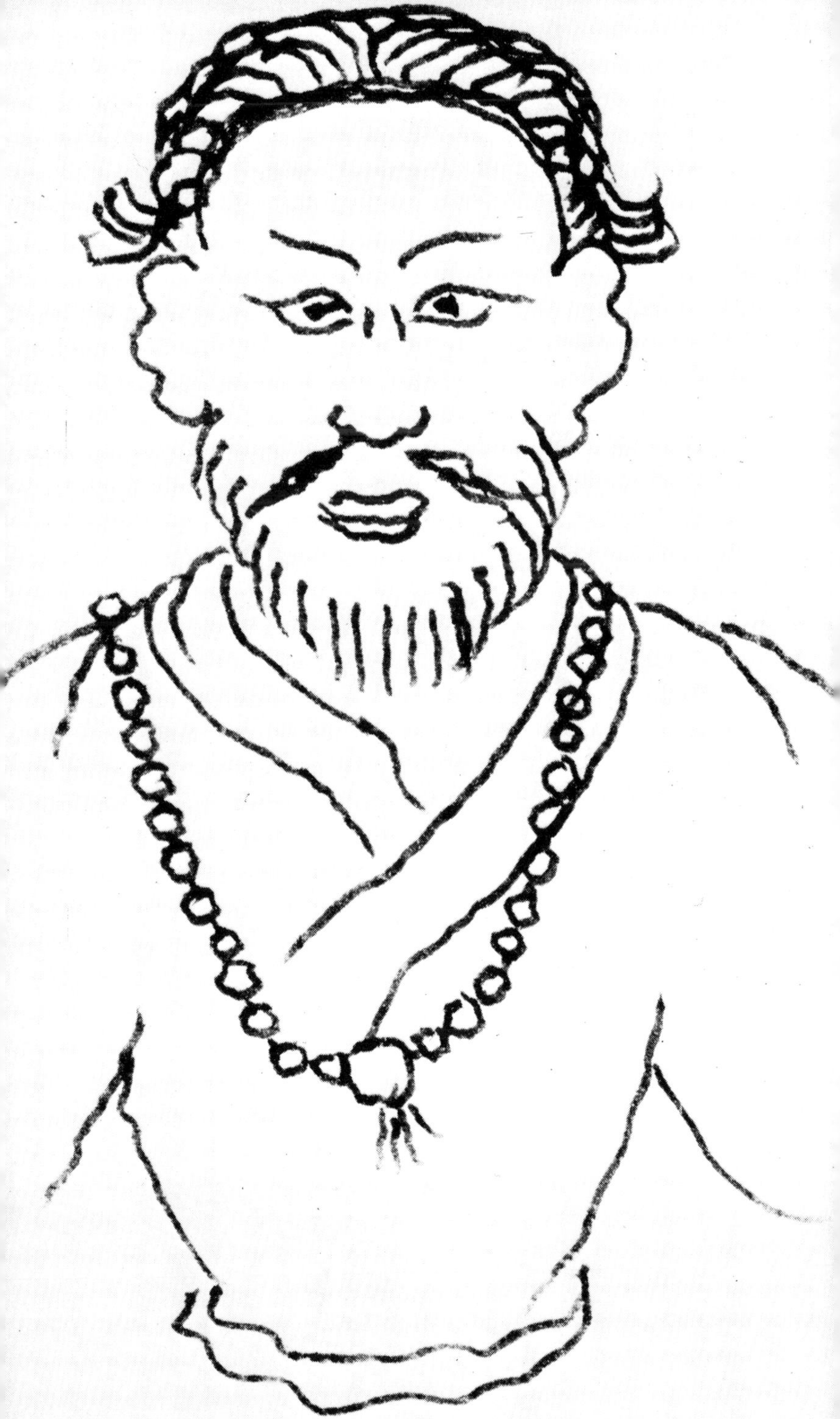